AFGHANISTAN SNIPER

AFGHANISTAN SNIPER

TRAUMA ON THE FRONT LINE AND BEYOND

TED SHIRLEY

FRONTLINE
BOOKS

AFGHANISTAN SNIPER
Trauma on the Front Line and Beyond

First published in Great Britain in 2025
by Frontline Books
An imprint of
Pen & Sword Books Ltd
Yorkshire - Philadelphia
Copyright © Ted Shirley
ISBN 9781036147617

The right of Ted Shirley to be identified as Author
of this work has been asserted by him in accordance with
the Copyright, Designs and Patents Act 1988.
A CIP catalogue record for this book is available from the British Library

All rights reserved. No part of this book may be reproduced or
transmitted in any form or by any means, electronic or mechanical
including photocopying, recording or by any information storage and
retrieval system, without permission from the Publisher in writing.

Typeset by Lapiz Digital
Printed and bound in the UK by CPI Group (UK) Ltd,
Croydon, CR0 4YY.

Printed on paper from a sustainable source by
CPI Group (UK) Ltd, Croydon, CR0 4YY

Pen & Sword Books Limited incorporates the imprints of
Archaeology, Atlas, Aviation, Battleground, Digital, Discovery, Family
History, Fiction, History, Local, Local History, Maritime, Military,
Military Classics, Politics, Select, Transport, True Crime, Air World,
Claymore Press, Frontline Publishing, Leo Cooper, Remember
When, Seaforth Publishing, The Praetorian Press, Wharncliffe Books,
Wharncliffe Local History, Wharncliffe Transport, Wharncliffe True
Crime and White Owl.

For a complete list of Pen & Sword titles please contact
PEN & SWORD BOOKS LTD
47 Church Street, Barnsley, South Yorkshire, S70 2AS, England
E-mail: enquiries@pen-and-sword.co.uk
Website: www.pen-and-sword.co.uk
or
PEN & SWORD BOOKS
1950 Lawrence Rd, Havertown, PA 19083, USA
E-mail: uspen-and-sword@casematepublishers.com

CONTENTS

List of Plates viii
Prologue x

Scotland. 1
Wales 9
The Stalk 14
The Night Nav 20
Kenya. 33
Pre-Deployment. 43
Afghanistan. 47
And Then There Were Four 53
The Enemy Sniper 58
The Longest Day. 63
Operation Moshtarak 71
The One-Mile Shots 79
Two Birds, One Stone. 84
Homeward Bound 89
The Armoury 92
PTSD 95
Just Do It 102
It's Time to Start Talking 109
Trust the Process. 112
Right, That's Enough. 115
Change is Scary 118
Holistic Healing 121

Sydney	123
The Farm	125
Counting Down the Days	132
Brisbane	135
Goodbye Australia	139
Portugal	142
Marge	147
Back to the UK	150
A Can of Worms	152
Forgiveness and Acceptance	156
DMT and Psilocybin	159
Back to Therapy	163
Doing the Work	165
Keep Going	169
Our Survey Says	172
Reflection	174
Index	184

'Nothing could have prepared me for what was coming next'

LIST OF PLATES

1. Me, Slater and Dan on an observation lesson in Brecon, south Wales.
2. Con, me and Andy just about to leave Camp Bastion with the Mobile Reconnaissance Force.
3. Me sat on top cover behind the grenade machine gun of our Jackal vehicle as we head through the desert to a target.
4. Me overwatching an enemy position as we take cover from Taliban fire in an irrigation ditch.
5. Bennie, Jenks, myself and Gray catching a quick photo before heading out on a strike op. Gray with a cat's arse sausage roll hanging out of his mouth.
6. Me and Dan in the back of a Chinook after an op.
7. Adi, Jenks and Bennie providing cover for troops as they extract out of enemy fire.
8. Me observing a potential enemy position as Estonian troops advance to investigate.
9. Gray scanning for Taliban fighters as ground troops advance into battle.
10. Bennie observing enemy movements from the shadows.
11. Jenks in his rooftop sniper hide.
12. Me on the rooftop of FOB Ddraig as Operation Moshtarak kicks off.
13. Me lying on the rooftop just before an RPG and AK-47 rounds got fired overhead.
14. After a long night of patrolling, me and the lads make it back to our FOB.
15. Me and some of the lads playing cards while we wait for something to happen.
16. After returning from a night recce and the rare chance I didn't have my trusty sniper rifle.

LIST OF PLATES   ix

17. A Chinook helicopter drops us off a much-needed resupply of food, water and ammunition. Except all the meals were bloody corned beef hash. Disgusting.
18. The mortar lads making a noise. This one I knew about.
19. Gray taking a knee as a chopper is inbound.
20. Me and Jenks smoking our cigars on the beach in Cyprus.
21. Me and Harry ride a tuc tuc through the streets of Bangkok.
22. Me and one of the boys soaking in the culture at a temple in northern Thailand.
23. A small jungle village in northern Thailand where we met the 'long neck' people of the local tribe.
24. Me and the gang dropping of some school supplies at a remote village in the jungle. We spent the next day helping to pick coffee beans with the farmers on the hillside.
25. Our little cabin on the sheep farm in Australia.
26. Me and the boys on a scorching hot New Year's Day in Brisbane. This is the second floor living room of our house.
27. Smashing out the tunes on the yacht while taking in the sights of Portugal's southern coast.
28. Me and the gang at the summit of a mountain in the Rockies of Canada.
29. Marge taking it all in as we stop off in America.
30. Me after breaking through the smoke barrier of wildfires. We camped over at the Yosemite National Park just below.

PROLOGUE

I was only 21 years old when I landed in Afghanistan for the second time. Except this time, things were different.

This time, I was a sniper, and nothing was going to stop me. There was a score that needed to be settled, and all the blokes had trained hard. You see, the sniper team had lost one of our own, and it was driving us like a pack of wolves on a hunt. Trained by the best and hungry for our revenge, these wolves were about to attack. But after the war, would we all come back? Or would we be lost to a world of darkness, violence and mental torture?

For security reasons, the names of some of the people mentioned in my story have been changed.

SCOTLAND

After a long drive up north, me and Dan finally saw the road sign that was pointing in the direction of what would be our new home for the next few weeks. The rest of the Welshmen, Gray, Bennie and Jenks, followed closely behind.

A run-down relic of a former WW2 base was our destination, which had now somehow been signed off to house the Direct Fire Divisions, Sniper Course.

Running along the rugged coastline of Scotland, with its difficult terrain and harrowing weather conditions, the location made for the perfect place to put this newly formed bunch of lunatics to the test.

Run by some of the British Forces' best snipers, civilian ballistics experts and notable veterans of wars not too far gone, this course was going to test everyone's wits, stamina, aptitude and determination, all while leaving no room for error.

The old red-brick buildings were in a tidy square formation at the old barracks, with a field in the centre, a small NAAFI bar, a cook house, and an armoury filled with shiny things and gadgets that we had never seen before. Our accommodation was made up of large twelve-man rooms, and each room consisted of a locker per man, a bed made up of as many springs as we could find knocking about on the floor, and a stinking green mattress.

We had our bags packed full of kit ready for our course. Combats, waterproofs and warm kit would make up most of it, accompanied by a set of PT kit, a set of fatigues for after hours, and a set of dancing shoes right at the bottom of our bags, just in case the opportunity arose. But let's face it, we always had a way of creating an opportunity to wear the dancing shoes.

The atmosphere in the rooms on that first cold Sunday evening was tense, to say the least, as everyone settled into their new homes. We had been hand-picked from various parts of the British Army and put forward for this extremely intense course. This opportunity, however, was not easily gotten, and we had all had to prove ourselves worthy for the chance to hold the revered title of sniper.

The first morning of the course started in the dark, and a cold, wet run over to the armoury was just what the doctor ordered to get us all wide awake and eager to get into a classroom for possibly the first time in some of our lives.

'Right, fellas,' shouted the sergeant major. 'Get yourselves ticked off on the register and make your way into the armoury to be issued with your weapon.' 'Tick ourselves off on the register?' we thought. 'Fuck me, I think we get treated like men here and not fucking kids,' whispered one of the guys at the back of the group that was standing waiting to go in.

Me and Dan looked at each other with excitement in our eyes as we headed in through the heavy steel doors of the dimly-lit armoury building.

'These are L96 Sniper Rifles, and you will all be issued with one, and you will treat it like it's your little fucking baby. They are not to be fucked about with or touched unless under either my or one of my directing staff's orders. Is that clear?' Shouts of 'YES, SIR!' echoed through the building.

Before arriving at the course, all of the men had to pass a vigorous pre-selection course, which had been orchestrated within their regiments. It's a hard course to pass, and only a very small percentage of the men sent there would walk away as a different type of soldier, an asset. A force multiplier, who could make life or death decisions in real-life situations.

The troops attending the sniper cadre had already been tested and had risen to the top. We were at the peak of our physical fitness and mental aptitude, but was it enough to see the course through until the end?

Days went by slowly at first, of seeing nothing but the inside of a classroom and listening to lessons on the theoretical science of shooting and ballistics. Staring at a blackboard filled with illustrations and calculations that were so intense and complex that they could nearly induce nausea.

The amount of detail that had to go into making a shot as a sniper was incredible. Learning how the elevation turret of a scope relates to the distance and learning how the inside rifling of a barrel affects the spin on a bullet, sending it to the right. We learnt about parallax in relation to the angle we were shooting at. We learnt about the wind and how it affects a round, and in turn, even calibrated ourselves to the wind. We learnt about how the little marks and mil dots inside of the scope picture all meant something, and how we could use them for various things. The list of subjects was extensive, and each came with their own complexities.

The learning curve was steep, and there was little to no chance of catching up if you fell behind the pace of the instructors. They were all experienced snipers and even master snipers. This meant a great deal to everyone, and everybody knew that to be a sniper, you had to be held to a high standard, and that standard was not going to be lowered for anyone.

As the days attended at the course added up, so did the number of troops who had been returned to their units. More and more each day would fall short, lose the grip they had on that infamous learning curve, and drift off back into the green machine that they had ascended from.

Finally, though, the time came to leave the classrooms and get our hands on the weapons that we now knew every single nook and cranny of. This section of the course was where the experience and expert advice of the training staff began to shape what would be the next draft of British Army snipers and potentially save our lives.

Learning the intricate details of what is involved in taking a shot as a sniper revealed that it was to be as beautiful and creative as it would be life-changing and gut-wrenching. Every scenario was played out over and over again. Every possible fire position was held until it hurt and then done again and again. The delicacies of balance and foresight. The ability to become one with the wind and to know all of its tricks. To send a round soaring through the sky, only to land exactly where we wanted it to. These were all just a small part of what it would take to become a sniper, but it was the foundation on which battle-ending, fear-inducing reapers would be made.

Weeks into the course, a brotherhood had begun to form, but not in the usual way. The military had a way of welding people together for life, and this course was beginning to do just that to the small number that remained. Only this time, it was through a love of being a sniper, and the more we learnt, the more we grew closer to each other. With the exception of the Welshmen, who had already bonded very early on in the course and now had our own internal agenda going on. To be better than the rest.

We had come together from two Welsh infantry battalions, and although we had never known each other before the course, there was an instant connection between us from our homeland, and we had all bunked up together in the same room.

Jenks, Dan, Gray, Bennie and myself, from one battalion, and Stevo, Slater and Warren, from the other battalion, had fought hard for our places on the course, and a lot was riding on us back at our battalions. We were to make up the newly formed sniper platoons at our units, and some of us had already received our orders to deploy to Afghanistan.

'Right, gents, listen in. Today, we're heading out to firing range number two. Grab your weapons and your kit, and get running,' shouted the Sergeant Major. 'Yes, Sir!' we shouted, and we quickly hit the road running.

The run was only a few short kilometres, but it was enough time for the nerves to set in about finally being about to fire the weapons. This was it; this was where all of those relentless days of lessons and practising various firing positions over and over again would come into play. However, it was all well and good knowing the theory side, but would everyone be able to achieve that level of professional accuracy with the shooting side that was required to go any further in the course?

As the first day on the shooting ranges progressed, it was apparent that not all would make the grade, and cuts were made yet again to the course. The Welshmen could hold our heads high though at the end of the day's shooting, and as we ran back to camp, morale was high, and so was our confidence.

Back in our room, it didn't take long for music to be heard, blasting out of the small radio that Jenks had brought with him, to listen to Talk Sport Radio as he slept. Quickly, the topic of the dancing shoes at the bottom of everyone's bags came up.

'Let's just hoof it over the little fence down by the gym and run into town, shall we, boys?' shouted Warren. 'Yes, here we go,' replied Bennie, eager for a beer. 'Fuck it, get dressed lads, let's do it,' I said, just as there was a loud knock on the door. 'Oi, you fuckers, get your kit on. You're doing guard duty on the main gate tonight, Roger,' said the voice on the other side of the door.

It was McCormack, an evil-looking man with an unnerving temperament. 'Yeah, no problem,' shouted Stevo, who already knew of him from his unit, as did Warren and Slater. 'Did we get busted then, or just dicked to do guard?' said Jenks. 'He'll of just dicked us for a guard, mate. He's deaf as a post, so he wouldn't have heard us talking about going out,' joked Slater. So we did as we were told and grabbed our kit, took off our dancing shoes, and headed over to the guard room for guard duty, which would last until the following morning. Watching gates and patrolling the perimeter fences all night while being housed in a tiny gatehouse with bunk beds and a Chinese takeaway telephone number.

'Have a good night, lads!' we heard shouted through the window of the gatehouse shortly after we arrived as a small bunch of guys from the course scurried out the gate with grins on their faces as they headed into town for the night. 'Bastards!' we all replied in unison.

The weeks went by on the shooting ranges, with shoots at varying distances and angles, from different fire positions, and in all types of weather conditions. We were getting better with every round we fired, and after a while, it had started becoming like second nature to us.

Laying behind that weapon day after day, in the rain and howling winds of the Scottish sea, was not an easy thing to do, but it did not seem to faze the Welshmen. Not now that we were so close to the end of our first phase of the course would we waver or fall. We had the skills required to make those difficult-to-make shots, and we knew our weapons well, and we knew that every one of us was as capable as the other on that firing range.

The daily runs to and from the ranges had now slowly turned into quick walks that were filled with questions for the instructors and personal insights into what life was to become, almost like unveiling a somewhat otherwise mysterious part of the armed forces that had been shrouded in secrecy and speculated on by those who wanted to be a part of the brotherhood and by fat men in corners of pubs.

Lessons were learned from the training staff's combined experiences, and advice was given from the old watch to the new, like warrior tales being passed on to encourage the younger generation.

As we made our way back to camp one crisp evening, the Sergeant Major joined us on the walk. 'Listen in, gents', he shouted. 'Tomorrow, we have a visitor coming to camp. This visitor will be here to determine whether or not snipers are still a viable asset to the British Forces out in Afghanistan and whether or not Government funding should be directed elsewhere. Now you lot are going to prove your fucking mettle tomorrow and show this prick that they don't know what they are talking about and that you lot are worth every penny that's spent on training you.'

The following morning was a cold and frosty one. The winds were gusting, and it wasn't going to be an easy day's shooting. We all headed to the armoury to collect our weapons as we did every morning, but today was slightly different.

A small section of soldiers had been brought up that day to demonstrate the power and functionality of a machine-gun group as compared to the extensive and expensive training of a sniper. They were met with the usual niceties of a group of squaddies meeting another for the first time, and then the big cheese came along. The government suit responsible for this inquest into the dark arts and the messenger back to the government what the results would be. Today, we would run to the ranges as we were joined by the machine gunners, but we wouldn't be going slow – we wouldn't want our new friends to get cold would we.

'Red flags up, crackled over the firing range warden radio. 'Right, everybody, listen in. Today, we will be firing from a range of 200 to 1,000 metres. Targets will fall when hit, and they will be popping up randomly at varying distances and elevations. Machine gunners, you're up first.' The team of eight machine gunners took their positions and loaded their belts of ammunition into their weapons, made ready, and waited for the first target to pop up. Four hundred metres, a target had popped up on a hillside, and one of the gunners let loose a burst of rounds, quickly followed by the rest of the team after seeing the splashes of his rounds hitting the dirt around the first target. A few seconds went by, and the target dropped down. Suddenly, three more targets popped up, and the machine guns team went to work. The sound of machine guns when they synchronise is music to the ears of anyone in a firefight. For just a moment, there is peace within it all. Another target popped up, and a bunch more. Dirt was being kicked up everywhere, and targets were going down, but that stopwatch was still rolling. Finally, the last target was taken down, and the gunners all breathed a sigh of relief. Next up, we're the snipers, and everyone was looking at each other as the names were called out of the snipers that would be firing that day. 'Jenks, Bennie, Ted, Dan, Gray, Stevo, Warren, Slater, you're up,' a voice said, coming over the range of speakers. We were in, and the pressure was on. We each took our positions without saying a word. We looked calm as we prepared our fire positions and peered over to each other's lanes, nodding as if to say, 'We've got this lads'. The first target popped up, Bang! Dan got it. Bang! I got the next. One after another, the targets dropped within seconds of popping up as the sniper team engaged them with ease. 'Eighteen seconds!' One of the directing staff called out. We had dropped every single one. Leaving the one minute twenty-five seconds it took the gunners as just a distant noise in the background, echoing through the hills. 'I think that answers your questions, Sir,' said the Sergeant Major. 'Right, lads, let's stop all this fucking about, shall we. Get yourselves back to camp. You've got tomorrow off.' We ran at the speed of a thousand gazelles back to camp elated, we busted out our dancing shoes, ready to celebrate our performance. Getting ready on a typical squaddie night out, especially with South Waliens, involved one tub of Spar wet-look hair gel being passed around the room, whoever had the most expensive aftershave would soon need a new bottle after everyone had their turn, and everyone would try each other's shirts on in an attempt to give themselves a new look depending whereabouts in the world we were. Stevo sorted out the taxi to meet us at the guard room, and within 30 minutes, we were off into the local town. Exhausted and still trying to process the magnitude of what we had just accomplished, we began to go from bar to bar. In the wake of a three-for-one special on some unbranded bottles of alcopops, we dispersed into the town's local nightclub, and Stevo was in his element. By some miracle, his distinct haircut and his taste in heavy music were just the trend in town, and he found himself in a sea of Scottish women, all intrigued by this young guy with a funny accent. Little did he know that some of these women had very furious-looking boyfriends standing in a ring around the dance floor watching him. But they didn't know that around them was a circle of men that had been cut from a different cloth. All of a sudden, a glass was thrown, and it smashed on the floor. Then, some pushing and shoving turned into a raging argument that spilt out onto the street. We all spread out just as a bottle was thrown from the now very large group of boyfriends and their friends, with Stevo in the middle of it all. Me and Dan looked at each other in the doorway of the club as we tried to slow down the flow of locals trying to join the action. Suddenly, a right hook was thrown, and it hit Stevo straight in his nose, and it was game time. Dan dived off the doorway steps to perform a flying head butt, which knocked one of the locals out cold as I chased a group of the local men up the street. The rest of the boys were handling the main group just as blue lights began to flash and reflect off the buildings. The locals ran for it, but we stayed where we were. In a millisecond, we had sobered up, and knew exactly what needed to happen next. 'They ran up there, officer!' shouted one of the lads. 'Be careful though, because they've got bottles, they've been throwing them.' 'OK, lads, thank you. You get yourselves off home now, you hear.' 'Yes sir, will do,' we all replied as they walked calmly out of sight and then we burst into tears laughing. A couple more pints in the pub down the road to cool off, and we headed back to camp, obviously accompanied by kebabs and chips.

Monday morning came around, and it was test week. We had had a well-deserved bit of time off over the weekend, and we were ready to take on our final challenge.

The final week would be all about our shooting abilities, and before long, we would know if we had made the cut or not. The potential snipers took up our positions on the numbered firing lanes as we waited for our instructions to come over the Tannoy system. 'Targets will fall when hit. In your own time . . . Go on,' shouted the Colour Sergeant and the final test of the course's shooting abilities had begun. Images of blackboards and classrooms flooded our heads as we locked into what the wind was doing and made the appropriate calculations. Each of us, without making a sound, knew exactly what we had to do, and we knew that we could do it. The firing range erupted like a crescendo of drums. The wind throwing the sound out to the ocean and surrounding hills. Our concentration was unbreakable. Our rifles had become an extension of our bodies, and we placed every round where it was meant to be, taking down every single target. As the last round was fired, suddenly we heard music playing. 'Today this could be the greatest day of our lives . . . ' blared over the range Tannoy speakers, and everyone turned around to hear Gary Barlow and Westlife playing as we all fell about the floor laughing. We had done it! We had passed Phase 1 of sniper training. Now, all that remained to do was clean our weapons, pack our kit and make the long drive home. We all felt a huge sense of achievement that day, and we all still feel it today.

However, a brief spell back at our units and we would be faced with our biggest challenge yet. Phase 2 sniper training in the hills of Brecon, south Wales.

WALES

By now, it had been some time since the Welshmen from the sniper course had been all together in one place. We had all gone away on various other courses in preparation for our deployment to Afghanistan, although we would not all be deploying together. Warren, Slater and Stevo came from a different battalion than the rest of us, and they had their orders. They had Colour Sergeant McCormack in their battalion, one of the training staff from Scotland, and he had continued to train them after Phase 1 to best prepare them for Phase 2, and for what would face them in the future. On the other hand, the rest of us Welshmen had Richie, a British Army master sniper who had been involved with multiple elite Special Forces around the world and their sniper training. With him came his civilian friend and ballistics expert, Ken. The pair devised a training regime that was to push us to our limits and beyond. We spent every opportunity we had out on the firing ranges, going through thousands of rounds week after week. To the point where a ten-pence piece at 1,000 metres was a 'gift', as Richie would say, as we tore multiple holes through the coins with ease. We learnt about exactly why bullets act the way they do and how certain factors can impact them. We had an extension of our training in Scotland, and this time, it was the stuff that your everyday soldier would not get to learn or practise. We were given free rein from the battalion and moved off in search of becoming the best we could be. We were brothers, and now it was time for us to prove our mettle once more, except this time on the dark mountains of the Brecon Beacons.

It was a rainy Sunday afternoon as we all pulled up in our cars to the guardroom in Sennybridge, a small tucked-away Army camp that was used for various units and courses, but for the foreseeable future, it was for the Snipers Cadre and the concurrent running SAS Selection. Again, it was a bare minimum camp, the same as Scotland, with the same old spring beds and leaky cold showers and roofs made of asbestos. The highlight of the place was the food in the cookhouse, which was nothing spectacular, but they never ran out of food, and it was always freshly made by a small group of lovely local ladies. Burning 4,000–5,000 calories a day was the norm for anyone staying in that camp, and we always made sure to thank the ladies for our food. Perhaps they gave a motherly energy that was more than welcome amongst most of the troops. Slowly, throughout the evening, guys started to show up in the dorm rooms somehow, the ones who lived the closest, though, arrived last as usual. This time, it was a different bunch of troops on the course, again from various regiments and units in the Army, but the Welsh boys were together again, and it made for a great first night catching up. That night, we sat on our beds, telling stories of what we had been up to since Scotland as we went through our kit together. Secateurs, gardening saw, waterproof pens and paper, a shammy leather. 'What the fuck have they made us buy all this shit for,' said Gray. 'Doing a spot of gardening while we're here, are we?' 'I'm sure we'll find out soon enough,' said Bennie, as he finished putting his new tape on his kit to stop any shines or reflections. All of a sudden, the door swings open, and Richie pops his head in. 'Make sure you don't forget anything tomorrow morning, gents, or you'll be in shit state. Believe me.' We all continued to double-check and pack our kit before going to sleep that night.

The following morning started at the crack of dawn, out on the parade square. Lined up on the edges of the concrete square stood us potential snipers and also the troops that were taking part in the SAS selection process. Rows of four-tonne trucks would soon whisk them away off onto the hills for their days of navigational exercise while we went about our day. Up pulled a couple of white minibuses just as we were being briefed on our first day's activities. 'Jump in fellas!' shouted one of the directing staff, Daz. A lance corporal from another unit who had been picked to be a part of the directing staff for our course. Mainly to set up the day's activities and to play a role in some of the exercises to come. He was a bubbly, friendly guy who made everyone on the course feel at ease and able to ask him any questions if we got stuck on anything. He was accompanied by two others, Macalister and Osborne, both from the same unit as Slater, Stevo and Warren. We grabbed our weapons and our kit and jumped onto the minibuses.

After a short drive, we arrived at the infamous training area where the first of many lessons on the course was set up and ready to begin as soon as it was light enough. The hills of Brecon seemed to have their own mysterious weather system that could switch from sun to snow in the blink of an eye. The buses pulled up only to be met by Richie and McCormack, who had been waiting there for us to arrive. 'Get lined up along here, gents, and get out your notebooks,' said Richie, who was the kind of guy who would, without question, go the extra mile to create the best snipers that he possibly could. The first lesson was quickly underway, and it was instantly captivating, although by now the rain had begun, which a lot of the time in Brecon would get you wet from the bottom up as it fell hard enough to bounce off the ground to some height. The lesson was on 'why things are seen' and techniques that we could use to spot objects or potential threats. Laying on the ground, we would have to draw a diagram of the area to our front and spot various objects that had been hidden there, ranging from 5 metres to 50 metres. It could be a piece of string or a single bullet casing, and as the rain pelted down onto our soaking bodies, we thought to ourselves how this was to be our new classroom, so we had better get used to it pretty quick if we were going to succeed. No matter how horrendous it got, we would be out in it, and usually on our stomachs. The day was filled with little insights into what makes a sniper a sniper. It wasn't just about the accuracy of our shooting, in fact, we quickly started to realise that the steep learning curve we had endured in Scotland to be able to shoot to that standard was just the tip of the iceberg. While it was going to come into play later in the course, the shooting side was just a small part of the whole package, and there was still a wealth of knowledge to learn. Lessons in camouflage and concealment became our obsession and an absolute necessity. We learned how using the intricate details of our ever-changing surroundings could blend us into any landscape. The famed ghillie suit, an old Scottish hunter's cloak used to disguise the human shape, would be attached to us at all times, but first they had to be 'weathered'. A time-honoured tradition in which potential snipers would crawl through the toughest of terrains for kilometres at a time on their stomachs through ditches and bogs, through sheep shit and razor-sharp grass. This, however, was a tough but necessary process, and after completing the 'weathering', we would then bury our ghillie suits in the ground to have their man-made materials look more natural and blend into our environment.

Days on the course were long, and the weeks seemed to go on forever. Morning after morning, we made our way to the parade square to catch the minibuses, and every morning, our bodies would be aching and bruised from the day before. The course was beginning to test our mental strength and physical endurance. Could we push ourselves through our pain barriers and our injuries and keep enough mental clarity to keep up with this whole new world of information that we must retain? Or would we break and be returned to our units and back to being riflemen? Day after day, the numbers would dwindle, just as day after day, the remaining snipers would see the rows of four-tonne trucks at the parade square shrink into just two. Sniper history had become a regular lesson by now in our day-to-day routines, and it built another layer of pride and ambition in us young men, who were now 20 years old for the most part. We learnt about the world's greatest snipers through the years and their tactics, soaking in every single detail like a sponge. Learning the history and techniques used by snipers through the years gave insight to us and also showed us that we had to be creative to become the best we could be.

To track down our targets, the art of 'stalking' would play a huge part in our roles as snipers, along with complex solo navigational skills. 'Stalking' was the process used by snipers to covertly move on an enemy position while remaining unseen, and it would incorporate every single lesson that we had been taught. Test week was not too far away, and it was beginning to show as the pressure continued to intensify. The Welshmen had again come together to ensure that every one of us was up to par and keeping up with the lessons. Again, we wanted to be the best we could be, not just for ourselves but for each other, so that we could keep each other alive. Late nights of studying and preparing mass amounts of kit for the following day's activities became the norm, and sleep became more of a luxury than a necessity. Days would usually consist of various lessons or mini tests and either a stalk or a navigational exercise, which would see us cover massive amounts of ground daily and usually by crawling. As the weeks went by, this became very typical for the remaining snipers, and soon we came to expect huge physically demanding insertions over difficult terrain, and our combat fitness was certainly fighting ready. Observing the landscapes and making note of features that could be used to aid navigation. Crawling for hours at a time through bone-scraping terrain and fly-blown bogs to reach final fire positions. Changing our camouflage as we moved and blending seamlessly into the backdrops of the hills and forests that surrounded us. After a time, we became invisible and extremely tough to track. We could live off the land in solitude for as long as was needed, all while being undetected by even the wildlife. Training began to intensify exponentially, and the attention to detail in every single thing we did had to be executed to perfection. Leaving no trace and being impossible to spot.

Soon, the stalks became longer and harder, as did everything else, and things were reaching that level of professional expectation that would be asked of us back at our units and on our upcoming tours to Afghanistan. One morning at the parade square, as we waited, two white vans hurled onto the concrete. Jerry cans filled with water and some Norwegian containers filled with the slop of the day range stew, also known as range poo, arrived at the our feet. 'Get in the back of the first van if your name is called out,' shouted Richie 'If it's not, then jump into the second van!' We listened for our names to be shouted and boarded our designated vans. Soon, we would find ourselves in total darkness as the van doors were slammed closed behind us. 'What the fuck is this then?' I laughed. 'Cheeky bit of escape and evasion, I reckon,' said Bennie. 'Nah, they just don't want us to see the burger van on the way up and have to stop, I bet,' said Jenks. The engines started, and the vans began to pull away, and we could only imagine what this sudden surprise meant. The sound of the cattle grid vibrated through the van 'Right, at least we know we're in the back area now,' said Dan. Every film, lesson, or book we had read was running through our heads. Trying calmly to count the turns and stops. Carefully listening to the ground underneath the tyres kicking gravel up on the underside of the van. By now, the sun had risen, and glimpses of light began to fill the gaps in the van doors, but not enough to see where we were. Just enough to be able to tell the difference between open roads and dirt tracks meandering through dense forests. All of a sudden, the brakes screeched, and the van came to a halt. We all grasped tightly to our weapons as we bounced around in the back of the van. We heard the front doors of the van open and close, then footsteps on the gravel moving towards the rear of the van. Pop, and the doors slowly opened. The early morning sun lit up the inside of the van, where one of the lads had taken a sneaky piss in the corner en route. 'Out you get,' said Daz. He then whispered, 'You're being tested today, lads, so be ready, OK?' with a wink. It was game time, and we knew it wasn't going to be easy.

'Right, men, listen in because I'm only going to say this once. You are about to be given a ten-figure grid reference. That grid reference is not to be forgotten and not under any circumstances to be shared with anybody!' One by one, we were taken aside and given instructions that only we would hear. And one by one, we quickly jogged off into the trees and faded into the countryside. Not a single one of us going in the same direction, and not a single one of us making a sound.

THE STALK

I had my grid reference fresh in my mind, and once I was deep in the cover of the forest, I stopped and knelt behind some cover. I pulled the map from my side pocket and began to scan the area surrounding me. Through the gaps in the wood block, I could see just the tips of some mountain features far in the distance. 'Right then, head up there a little, and I should be able to figure out where the fuck I am,' I thought. Looking around, I could see plenty of natural foliage which could be used to camouflage myself. I knew that nearer to the edge of the forest would be greener than it was deep inside, so I gathered up the green moss and ferns which surrounded me and began to stick them all over my kit, weapon and ghillie suit. Finally, after applying camouflage cream to any exposed skin, I took a swig out of my water bottle, and it was time to move. I knew I would be nowhere near the enemy position at the grid reference given to me, so for right now, that was not my main concern. I needed to find out where I was first, and then I could plan my route towards the enemy position and, more importantly, my final fire position.

The light started to become brighter as I carefully made my way towards a break in the treeline, which would give me the best view of the landscape. I took out my map and began to use its contour lines to determine which mountains they were that I had seen and which valley it was that I could now see below me. Triangulation is the method used to find out your current location, using recognisable features in the land and their bearings to lead to a point on the map and, in turn, your location. All of the hours spent in classrooms and on soaking-wet grass listening to the complex equations needed to perform such a wizard-like navigational master class. All of the late nights sat on the end of our beds, studying everything we had been taught. It was all for this moment. I was never any good at mathematics, and I knew it. However, this was different. This I cared about, and this was about my dream.

All of a sudden, two Lynx helicopters flew over the valley, heading to the southern training area where something snazzy was going on, and it filled me with adrenaline as I prepared for my descent into the valley. In the safety of the permanent darkness at the edge of the forest, I studied my map, the grid reference given to me circulating in my mind. A quick swipe of my fingers against the waterproofed map, and I had it. The enemy position was at the edge of a treeline. It was at a lower elevation, down the valley and around its dark and misty bend. 'If I just follow this valley down and around, then it's a pretty straightforward shot, but there's a chance I could be seen,' I thought. I sat for a moment and thought of every single detail that I could. The wind, the weather that looked like it was about to chuck it down any minute, the direction of the moving sun. So many things had to be assessed and planned for this to be a successful stalk. 'The valley is my best option,' I thought. 'I'll move down into the valley and along the bottom through the stream. There's plenty of big rocks and bushes down there to use for cover.' Up on the far side of the valley sat another forestry block, this time not as dense as the one I had just passed through but still a good location with plenty of cover. The trees were taller but much more sparse, with thinner trunks, which meant I would have to be careful not to silhouette myself. Looking at the moving sun, I could see that it was heading in the direction of the skinny forest on the hill opposite me. 'That's what I'll do,' I said to myself. 'Down this valley, through the stream, and then up the other side just before the bend. That way, I can use that forest as a backdrop.' The sun was going to move directly behind the woods where I intended to find my final fire position. Making a direct line from the sun, through the forest, through me, and onto the enemy position, it was perfect. With the sun shining in their eyes, the enemy would never be able to see me. I began my descent down the slippery valley slope, doing my best not to spook any of the sheep that were grazing not too far away from me. Each step was taken carefully so as not to disturb the loose rocks or slip on the wet moss. On reaching the stream, it turned out to be a little wider and a little deeper than it had first appeared from my vantage point at the top of the valley. I had covered 5 kilometres by the time I reached the water's edge, and throwing my 85lbs kit over to the other side of the stream came as light relief from the weight just before plunging into the icy water to get over to the other side. A quick dip up to my waist, followed by a short few steps, and I pulled myself out of the water. The water was so cold that it had already begun to freeze my muscles into place, which meant I needed to move quickly. My feet were numb as I flung my heavy kit back onto my aching shoulders and started the difficult climb up to the top of the valley. Sweat streamed down my face as I wiped my brow to clear what remaining camouflage cream was left on my forehead before it ran into my eyes.

I could see the tops of the trees peering over the valley top as I edged closer, now it was time for the details to be planned. I stopped before I would reveal myself on the horizon, taking cover in a big fern bush. I took out my map and checked again the position of the target. I peered around the corner of the valley and could see the forest block in which the instructors would be sat at the enemy position, eagerly scanning the area with their binoculars, looking for snipers on the move. As I scanned the area, I could see men in high-visibility vests walking around, and they were holding a radio and a big high-visibility cardboard arrow each. I put away my map, 'Up here all sneaky peaky-like, and then I'll crawl up into the edge of the forest,' I thought to myself. There was an area just at the edge of the forest, tucked away in the permanent shadow cast by the trees. It was full of broken tree limbs, moss, and various tall grasses and ferns. It was the perfect spot for my final fire position. Good cover from view and fire, and it would give me a great spot to engage the target.

This was to be a blank firing exercise, and the details of such an exercise had already been explained to the snipers earlier in the course to prepare us for when the day came. The guys all thought that it would be the last week of the course precisely, but we were wrong. The instructors had brought the test week forward by a few days. The men in the high-visibility vests were Daz, Macalister and Osborne. Their role that day after dropping us lot off in the vans was to spread out within a pre-determined acceptable range of the target and wait for a sniper to fire a shot. They would then move towards the general area of that sniper, completely ignoring any other snipers they might encounter so as not to give away their position. Once in place, the staff member would radio through to the instructors at the target, and they would then proceed to investigate the area in detail using their binoculars, searching for the sniper while holding up a letterboard. If the instructors think they have spotted the shooter, then they simply radio through to the walkers and guide them in to point the arrow at the presumed sniper's head. If they fail to spot him on that first attempt, the sniper is then clear to engage again and fire another shot. This is where it gets tough. The sniper must fire a second shot and not be seen doing so, all while the enemy is searching for him in his general location. If the enemy position fails to spot the sniper again, then they must stop looking for him at that point, and the sniper can then begin his covert extraction.

Peering up at the glistening sun, it was now starting to break through the clouds, I could envision my route into my final position using the shadows. I began to leopard crawl up the hill, my belt buckle scraping the dirt and my heavy kit tied to my right leg, dragging it carefully behind me. My rifle was resting over my shoulder as I held it with the web of my right hand. This enabled me to crawl lower and allowed me to painstakingly grasp onto the blades of grass and drag myself along at the pace of a snail, inch by inch, up to my final position.

I reached the edge of the wood line and tucked myself away deep into an opening in a large prickly bush. I had to be careful not to sway the branches above me and attract the eagle eyes of the instructors. I could see my final fire position ahead. Dark and well-covered, it made for the perfect location to fire from. It would also make for an easy withdrawal back into the cover of the forest for my extraction. I studied the land, watching for any signs of movement or any possible wildlife that might give away my position. It was all clear, and so I began to change the natural camouflage that I had used earlier that morning to disguise my shape. Intricate details were not too much to ask in this situation. Every single leaf could be the difference between success and failure. I applied my camouflage cream for the final time and used some to cover up the silver ring at the muzzle end of the old L96 barrel. Every colour and texture had to match my surroundings, and I had to be covered from head to toe in foliage to become invisible. Inch by inch, I began to make my way over to the broken tree limbs and rocks in front of me, moving out of the thorny bush in slow motion while being in a state of hypervigilance. Slowly, I reached my final position and began to blend myself seamlessly into the area. 'Get yourself comfy, mate,' I thought to myself as I lay behind my weapon, nestling myself into the ground as low as I could. I began to cover myself in ferns and sticks, which made up the majority of my cover. Once I was confident in my camouflage, I flicked open my sight covers and began to scan the area across the valley to my front. There it was, after only a quick scan of the area, I could see the enemy position, with Richie and McCormack both sitting there peering through their binoculars, searching for snipers. They were about 650 metres away, not a difficult shot to make for a sniper, and within the predetermined designated firing area. I began to calculate all of the elements I needed to. 'Five clicks elevation,' I whispered to myself. 'Five clicks left because that wind is whipping around the corner of the valley, and I'm shooting slightly downward,' I thought. I dialled in the adjustments to my scope and observed the wind in the trees and the elephant grass. Slowly, I flicked off my safety catch and began to draw long, deep breaths in and out. Slowly reducing my heartbeat to a fraction of its speed was by now something I was well-practised in, and once I had reached an almost meditative state, I was ready. I peered through my scope at the instructors sitting in their hide, oblivious to my position. I began to squeeze the hand grip of my weapon tightly and then very slowly release the pressure of each finger individually, as if I were playing the piano. It was a trick that Richie had taught us so that we would consistently hold the weapon and squeeze the trigger with the same amount of pressure every time we fired. Even the slightest of details would influence how a round was released from the barrel and flew soaring through the sky. The minutest discrepancy or error made at my end would be multiplied exponentially as the bullet covered more and more distance, and so everything had to be perfect.

As I took my aim at one of the instructors and continued to slow my breathing down further, the crosshairs of my weapon began to slowly move up and down in a perfectly straight line, straight through my target, up and down, up and down. I squeezed the trigger, and the shot rang out, echoing through the valley, as a small plume of steam came from the muzzle of my rifle due to the cold, damp air in the forest. I lay perfectly still, not even moving to breathe for a moment. All was silent through the forest, and then, moments later, I heard the snap of a twig behind me. Daz appeared in his yellow vest, holding the high visibility cardboard arrow, and he was making his way towards me. I stayed perfectly still, eager to fire my second shot and get the fuck out of there, but I still had to wait and see if I had been spotted by Richie or McCormack. 'Forward ten steps, right three steps', I heard coming over Daz's radio. Daz moved forward and to the right. 'Yep, right there,' the voice on the radio said. The arrow was pointing at a rock 15 feet away from my position, which came as a huge relief. 'Miss,' Daz replied and lifted his arrow, quietly saying, 'Sniper, you are clear for your second shot.' I slowly pulled back the bolt of my rifle and caught the ejected round casing in my fingers. A cool trick that had been practised a lot during our time in Scotland. I chambered my next round and aimed. The wind conditions hadn't changed, and so I proceeded to take the shot. Again, the sound echoed through the Valley, and this time, birds flew up from the trees throughout the valley. Suddenly, another shot was fired in the distance. It was one of the other lads taking their first shot from somewhere over the other side of the valley. 'Ten steps forward,' came over the radio. Daz started to move. 'And ten steps left,' said the voice on the radio with confidence. I shut my eyes and just hoped they were wrong. I could hear footsteps getting closer but dared not move a muscle to look closer and closer; they grew, and then they stopped. Frozen with the implications of what that arrow landing on my head could mean, I stayed perfectly still. 'Miss,' Daz replied on the radio. I'd done it, and now the instructor's eyes were busy looking out for whoever fired that other shot. Daz approached my position and proceeded to check with me what letter was being held up on the board and the adjustments I had made on my sights to make sure that the shot would have landed on target. 'Yep, that's all spot on that, mate, well done. Now make your way to the extraction point, which is at grid 4567674534.' 'Roger mate, cheers,' I said, as I gave a light sigh of relief. I slowly began to crawl backwards out of my position and into the cover of the deeper dark forest behind me. I checked my map and slowly set off to my extraction point. A couple of kilometres and I had made it to the stone track which led to the car park. The minibuses were there, and so were the Norwegian containers full of range poo and 'cofftea', a brown brew-like liquid that was neither tea nor coffee but some kind of hybrid mixture because of the many years of use, but at least it was warm, and that was very welcome.

One by one, the sniper recruits arrived at the car park, all returning from their stalks dripping wet and frozen to the bone. Covered from head to toe in cuts and bruises from putting our bodies out of our minds in order to achieve what we needed to achieve. Drained from the exercise and looking forward to heading back to camp, we all lit up cigarettes and shovelled down the range stew that had been sitting around all day. As the last of the snipers arrived, we all sat on the ground using our kit to sit on as a barrier from the puddles and as we spoke about our day. 'OK, gents, listen in,' said McCormack as we all glanced over with a side-eye. 'Some good work there today fellas. Some not so good. But now, because I am such a kind and generous man, I'm going to allow you to correct that. Tonight, you will be conducting one of your final night navigational exercises.' 'What the fuck,' one of the lads muttered under his breath as most of us rolled our eyes discreetly. 'You will all be given a set of grid references, which will lead you to checkpoints. These checkpoints will be manned by your directing staff, and they will provide you with a password correlating with your name. They will not be easy to spot, and just like yourselves, they will not be using torches, this is a tactical exercise. Be mindful of your time because you'll have to fucking shift it if you're going to make the allotted time to pass this test. Right, fill up your water bottles and standby for your name to be called out.' 'Fuck me, man,' said Dan. 'I know, mate, shit this,' I replied. 'Least we'll get a good kip tonight', I joked.

THE NIGHT NAV

One by one, our names began to be called out, and each lad threw their kit over their shoulders with a heavy thud and squelched off into the night as the last bit of sunlight came from behind the hills. There was a new moon over the training area that night, and it seemed like just a small tear in the dark blue sky. The stars began to twinkle through the occasional gaps in the heavy grey clouds. A few more minutes and there would be no light at all to guide us through the night. On night nav exercises, it was mandatory to have a small 2cm glow stick attached to the back of our kit so we could be seen more easily with night vision for safety purposes. The terrain was ever-changing underfoot, and the loose rocks and shingles would make moving up and down hills difficult. Dense woods and knee-deep bogs would slow us down to a fraction of the speed we needed to be moving. Open fields would be the only way to move fast enough to make the time. There was not a moment to spare, and so given the opportunity, each of us would run as fast as we could through the darkness. We were trained not to use roads or obvious routes, and tonight, there would be vehicle patrols on the lookout for us.

Halfway through the night and several kilometres in, I had stopped to check my map in a ditch. 'What's that?' I thought as something caught my eye in the distance. A small, barely visible glow appeared in the night mist that appeared to be a small glow stick. The mist had started to grow, bringing an unwelcome freeze to the air that night. 'Who's that?' I whispered, to which I got no reply. 'Oi ya cunt!' I said louder, in case they couldn't hear me. Still, there was no reply. The dark, misty nights on the hills could be a very lonely place, and it was just as much of a test for our minds as it was for our map reading skills. I slung my kit over my shoulder and moved towards the glow, hoping to have a quick chat and a morale boost with one of the boys. 'Oi', I called out as I approached the light. 'Who's that?' I said, 'Stop fucking about.' The light moved away and headed off towards the middle of an open field. I followed, and foolishly, all thought of the navigational exercise went out of my mind for a moment. I was a jokester, as were all of the Welshmen. 'I'll sneak up and frighten the life out of them,' I thought to myself with a grin on my face. I began to jog quietly behind the light as it moved at a similar pace away from me. I ran faster and faster, jumping over tall grass and thorny bushes and then suddenly the light stopped, and I bolted towards it, thinking about how funny this was about to be when I caught whoever it was, that was until the light moved again, back and forth next to a bush erratically as I got closer and closer.

'You've got to be fucking kidding me!' 'No way!' I said out loud. The light I had been following had not come from a glow stick at all, but it had been coming from a fucking glow worm. I couldn't believe it, and suddenly, all thoughts of the exercise came flooding back into the forefront of my mind. 'Shit! Where the fuck am I?' I thought. I dropped my kit onto the ground, and the cold air went straight up my shirt, which was soaked to my back. I knelt and pulled out my map. The mist had now turned into a thick fog that had surrounded me, and it was getting worse by the minute. The sky was filled with heavy clouds, and the small slither of a moon that dimly lit the ground earlier was no longer visible. The fog crawled slowly along the freezing ground towards me like something from a horror movie. I looked all around, but there was nothing to see, nothing but grey. 'Shit, I'm fucked here,' I thought. 'Right, head back towards that ditch,' I said to myself, and I started to move my freezing body, which by now was stiff from the cold and wet. Most ditches in the area meant that there was some kind of feature nearby that I could use. As I reached the ditch, I could just about make out the top of some trees a few hundred metres away, and I changed my direction and headed directly for them, hoping to maybe, by sheer luck, find a checkpoint as this was a common location for them to be hidden away. As I picked up speed towards the forest, I began to run. The time I had lost because of this situation would quite possibly lead to me failing the test, and that was all I could think about. I ran as fast as I could, then suddenly Bang! I hit the floor. The training area in Brecon was renowned for these little bastard, hard, ball-shaped mounds of soil and grass known as 'baby heads' to those that were familiar with the place. I had hit one, and it had taken me growling in pain to the floor. The weight of my heavy bergen landed on top of me, and my rifle caught me on the chin as I went down. I lay there, defeated and in pain. Biting my bottom lip, I stared into the night sky. 'Fuck, man! Get up, mate,' I said to myself. With a deep breath, I drew all the strength I could muster and pushed off the ground, grasping at the grass between my fingers to help me to my feet. I stumbled backwards but quickly gained my balance. As I started to walk it off, I spotted something. It looked like a bunch of stones just through the fog. 'That's got to be a road,' I thought. I moved hastily towards it. 'Yes!' I said out loud. It was a road, and now I had a choice to make. Use the road and potentially be caught, or head back into the soaking wet, foggy marshland I'd just worked so hard to get out of. I checked my watch.

The faint green light of my Casio lit up my face. I was too late. I'd missed the cut-off time for the test, and so I had failed. I was gutted and knew that this could be devastating. But that was not all. I was still lost, or 'navigationally embarrassed', as Richie would say. Right now was a real serious situation that I had to figure my way out of. I didn't know where I was, and I was now in danger of becoming hypothermic. It was not at all uncommon for men to go down with hypothermia on these hills, and I did not want to become one of them while moving alone at night. 'Fuck this. I'm running down this road,' I said as I began to slowly pound my numb, wet feet into the hard gravel road. Every step sent shocks up my spine, and my ankle was swelling from the baby's head fall earlier and causing me a lot of pain.

I loved to sing. It was something I had done from a very young age, and so that's just what I did. I began to sing out loud as I kept the timing of the song with my feet. I knew that 'Bat Out of Hell' by Meatloaf was about ten minutes long, so I sang the song over and over to help with my timing and pace, but also my morale. I ran down the road without slowing down one bit; I wanted to finish strong. Even if it was mostly for myself, as I passed wood block after wood block, I started to recognise where I was. The road led to a spot in the training area called Dixie's Corner. A place the snipers had used a lot throughout the course, and it was just around the next corner. I pulled the straps of my kit tight and adjusted my clothes as I approached the end of the nav ex, where the rest of the men would be by now. I turned the corner and could make out the vans, surrounded by the rest of the guys. As I got closer, Richie shouted out to me. 'Ted, what the fuck happened, lad?' I threw my head back in disappointment, and I told him about everything that had happened. 'Fucking tough out there tonight, mate,' Bennie said. 'Yeah, bro,' I replied. 'A few of the lads aren't back yet, mate,' Dan said, who hadn't arrived much earlier than me. He'd had a little mishap himself during the night and ended up leaving a piece of kit behind at a checkpoint, meaning he had to double back on himself for quite some distance. A brew and a smoke as the rest of the guys made it back, and everything was starting to wind down. Richie and McCormack were disappointed, and they didn't hide it. 'Get in the buses,' said

McCormack. We got to our seats quickly and quietly. He was not the kind of man you wanted to piss off. The journey back from the night nav was quiet. The heating had steamed up all of the windows on the bus, and most of the troops fell asleep, exhausted from the toughest day of the course so far. As we arrived back at camp, Richie spoke up. 'Right, fellas, get in and get your weapons cleaned and back into the armoury and then I suggest you get your head in the books tonight, ready for tomorrow morning. Sniper history test, followed by your final observation and panoramic drawing tests. Fucking gift!' And with that, he left, and we headed back to our rooms.

The sniper cadre was as tough physically as it was mentally, and right now, we were feeling just how tough of a course it was. But this was just the beginning of test week, and several tests remained, including another night navigation test. We all sat on our beds, cleaning our weapons as huffs and puffs filled the room. 'Fuck this lad,' Gray said. 'Who's coming for a smoke?' 'Yeah, mate' a bunch of us replied. 'How are we feeling about tomorrow, lads?' I said. 'Yeah, easy, mate,' said Jenks.

The lads all knew their sniper history. We loved to learn it and hear the stories of snipers from around the world throughout the years and how they had influenced sniping as we know it today. The different weapon systems and tactics used, and we could see the history in what we had learnt ourselves. We weren't worried about that test. But the observation test was never going to be easy.

The following day started early as usual, but the aches and pains in our bodies were now so painful that they had become almost funny. Laughing at how each other could barely move without letting out a moan or a groan and the unmistakable scent of deep heat in the air.

The SAS had finished their hills phase and headed off to the jungle, so camp was left empty, with just us snipers dining in the cook house that morning. A quick five-minute feed and we headed outside and up to the classroom for our first test of the day. 'Shit. My mind just went blank,' said Stevo, 'I can't remember any of it,' he said with a worried look on his face. 'You'll be fine, butt,' said Warren, as Slater laughed uncontrollably. Everyone started to laugh, and we reached the classroom in high spirits. 'Right, sit the fuck down,' said Richie. 'Fucking gift this one, fellas. You'll be given a test sheet, and all you have to do is answer the fucking questions. Easy,' he said with a smile on his face. Richie was a Yorkshireman, and would often come out with some hilarious one-liners that would be circulated throughout the day by the Welshmen. They liked Richie, and he had taught them all a lot. But it was still fun to take the piss out of him.

The test began, and before long, we were looking around the room, scratching our heads. we were exhausted and giddy, and we soon all burst out laughing at each other, being 'in clip', which was army slang for a lot of things, but mostly that someone was struggling with something. After a quick telling-off from Richie, we put our heads down and continued with the test.

Pretty soon though, we were all finished, and it was time for the next test, so we headed back to our rooms to collect our kit for the day out on the training area. The panoramic sketching and observation tests were at least not physically demanding, but they did require intense concentration over long periods. First up was the observation test, which was by now something we had been doing for weeks, over and over, along with a huge list of other practices. The test went by without a hitch, and the snipers moved to our next location via the minibuses.

A hilltop grassy verge would be our spot for the next few hours, overlooking the hills and valleys in front of us. For most, this was the green grass of home, and it would soon become a part of us that would be looked back on with the fondest of memories. We took our positions on the ground and began to pull out our drawing folders. Something that had become an arts and crafts obsession among the Welshmen, designing pen holders and flaps to protect the paper from the rain. It had become standard for us to lay on the cold, wet ground inside our waterproof sleeping bag covers. Our one focus right now was the landscape in front of us and how we would draw it to the very best of our abilities. Our panoramic sketches had to include intricate details and also be true to scale, as well as include the distances between us and key features in the drawing.

We had been trained by this point to the highest of standards, and this, in turn, came with its responsibilities. As a sniper, one of our main roles was to overlook enemy positions and gather intelligence while working closely with reconnaissance units. We would now have the ear of those way up high in the chain of command, enabling us to trump decisions made by our commanding officers if needed. As well as providing invaluable details of routes, enemy movements and any potentially battle-winning or losing details. This was why the test was so important. We had to prove that we were responsible enough and capable enough to stand firm in our decisions and provide accurate details.

The stopwatch began, and we all fell silent as we began to draw. There never seemed to be enough time to fully complete previous sketches, but this had led to a natural sense of urgency in us and before long, we had all finished drawing. 'Up you get, fellas!' shouted Richie. 'Hand your drawings into Daz and get your kit packed away as fast as you can. We've got plenty of stuff to get squared away today.' We moved quickly and handed in our test papers to Daz, who acknowledged the good work the we had all put into our sketches. After a quick smoke, we jumped onto the buses and hit the road.

On the way back to camp, both buses were briefed on what was next to come by the directing staff. 'OK, lads, it's final ex time,' said Daz. 'Tomorrow morning is going to start with an eight-mile insertion tab with a full sniper OP kit. It will be timed, so it will count as your combat fitness test for the course. However, you will be significantly overweight with all the extra kit, but the one hour, fifty-five-minute cut-off still stands.' 'Fuck sake, here we go,' said Gray. Gray's nickname was 'Mantress'. Half man, half mattress, and he hated physical tests, even though he'd pass them with ease. Daz turned around to face us from the front seat of the bus. 'As soon as we get back to camp, head over to your blocks and get your kit prepped for the morning lads. You'll be out for a few days on your observation post-test, so make sure you bring everything you need and get a fucking good breakfast in you because this is the toughest one yet. Just keep focused and remember why you're here, OK,' he ended in a caring tone. A few minutes later, the buses pulled up in camp, and we headed back to our rooms for the night.

The following morning started in the dark, and we headed to the cook house to get our 'fucking good breakfast'. Fried bread, topped with baked beans and oily fried eggs, was the usual hot breakfast choice. Accompanied by fatty bacon and grisly sausages, the whole breakfast would be taken down using bread slices as cutlery. Just trying to take on as many calories as we could as for the next few days we would be eating nothing but cold rations.

The OP test would consist of the 8-mile run, carrying around 100lbs of kit, straight into digging and hiding an observation post. A position would be built underground through into the night. The snipers would have to build a well-camouflaged hide, where we could watch a target that would be identified by a grid reference given to us by the staff on completion of the Combat Fitness Test march. The hide had to be invisible, so that meant no lights whatsoever, which meant no smoking, no hot food, no hot drinks, and not being able to see a thing underground after dark. We would live entirely underground for the next few days in an 8-foot by 8-foot wide and 4-foot deep hole in the ground. Having nothing but a hole at the back to enter through and a tiny rabbit burrow-sized hole at the front to watch the target. This is where we would observe, take notes, man the radio, and draw a panoramic sketch of the area, which we would all take turns to add to as the days and nights progressed. Swapping position every 2 hours, we would man this OP in total silence and complete darkness. Every single item we took in with us had to leave with us. This meant that we needed to know exactly where everything was placed in our kit, to the point where we could find everything with our eyes closed. Feeling our way in the dark while shitting in bags and pissing in bottles that all had to be stowed away in our kit. Without being able to see. There was a reason why sniper training is so often spoken about and speculated upon, and this test was the subject usually being talked about. The directing staff came into the cookhouse and shouted, 'Outside, fellas.' We shovelled the rest of our food into our stuffed mouths and hastily made our way outside to meet the minibuses. The buses would take us up deep into the training area and drop us off at our start point for the timed insertion TAB or 'Tactical Advance into Battle'.

The brakes screeched as the buses came to a halt on the gravel road. 'Out you get boys,' said Daz. We all jumped out and threw on our kit. McCormack was going to lead the insertion run, and he had no intention of taking it easy. The route consisted of mostly hills, and underfoot would be gravel roads the entire way. All of a sudden echoed, 'By the left, double march!' And McCormack began to run, sending us scrambling across the gravel to catch up with him. He was running as fast as he could and didn't seem to be slowing down any time soon. We eventually all caught up and moved into formation, three ranks of single file. The run was silent mostly, except for the odd moan or groan from a twisted ankle. Halfway, everyone had warmed up and was in a good rhythm to complete the run comfortably, all except for Stevo. He had woken up starving that day and wasted no time in the cook house devouring as much food as he could, and that boy could eat.

As the pack began to spread out and the sweat began to pour from our heads, we had all started to really dig deep and go to that place in our minds to get through it. I had fallen to the middle of the pack, and suddenly, a stitch in my side hit me like a freight train. I was cramping up and was forced to stop for a moment as the rest of the men passed me. I took a quick sip of water and caught my breath at the side of the road while trying to calm the stitch in my side. As I recovered, I noticed Stevo was way behind the group. I could tell that he was struggling, and things didn't look too good for him. I started to run towards him just as the 'Jackwagon' turned around the corner. The Jackwagon would creep behind troops at a pace quick enough to just make the time, but if you fell behind it, then you were done. 'Come on mate, let's fucking move,' I shouted. 'You alright?' I asked, concerned.

'I'm fucked, mate,' Stevo replied. 'That bastard breakfast has done me right in, mate.' I could tell that Stevo's mind was starting to slip, and he was losing focus. He needed help, and with that, I grabbed him by the arm and started to drag him down the road just enough to get his legs moving. We had been in this together from the start, and none of us were being left behind this close to the end. As I shouted words of encouragement at Stevo, the rest of the Welshmen who were leading the pack turned to see what the noise was about. They could see me pulling Stevo along as he used every last bit of energy he had to try to finish the run. There was just one mile to go when the Welshmen at the front suddenly all stopped and started to run back up the hill towards Stevo and myself. McCormack screamed, 'What the fuck are you doing! Get here with me now.' But the Welshmen steamrolled their way in the opposite direction. They were a wolf pack, and absolutely nothing was going to stand in their way. 'Let's go, mate! We've got this. The finish is just around that corner!' They shouted as me and Stevo reached the pack and Stevo was pushed up to the front of the group. The idea that every single one of those men had put themselves on the line for him had spurred Stevo on, and he used that to drive himself forward, and the pack finished the test as one unit.

We dropped our kit at the side of the road and took out our water bottles. 'Well done, men,' said Richie, who was standing with a clipboard. 'OK, listen in. You'll be split into groups, and then you'll be given a grid reference for each of the team's target locations. Once you've been given your grid reference, you need to make your way to your OP position, which will be given to you by your directing staff.' We all separated into our given sniper teams and began to plan our route to our observation post locations with the overwatching eye of the instructors.

The Welshmen were teamed up together and quickly established which route we would take, and within a couple of minutes, we were on our way. It was a 2-kilometre approach through treelines and dense woods until we reached our approximate destination. The enemy position was nearby, and we needed to identify it quickly and then select our final OP position. A quick look down into the valley, and we spotted the target. A white farmhouse at the end of a long track, surrounded by small outbuildings with a Land Rover parked outside. As soon as we spotted it, we made our way deep into the forest, which was sitting at the top of the hill looking down over the farmhouse. The forest was dark and damp, with thick cover overhead from the canopy of giant oak and sycamore trees. A thick layer of moss grew over almost everything inside the forest like a freshly-fitted carpet. We quietly and slowly made our way to the location that would become home for the next few days.

A built-up natural defence of thick soil and bushes made for the perfect location to begin our dig. We placed our kit in a neat pile on the ground and took out our entrenching tools and secateurs. We marked out the area which we would be digging and began the arduous task of removing all that dirt. Hours went by of tactical digging, which meant a lot of time on our knees and having at least one man on lookout at the rear and one watching the target. The work was hard, but we soon had the dirt and rocks out of the space. We used the dirt and rocks to build up a defensive position and blended it into the surroundings. The observation post was starting to take shape, and we quickly checked that there was enough room for all of us and our kit to fit inside. Next, we moved onto the roof built by gathering fallen trees and branches, which would be laid over the top of the large hole. Then dirt, sticks and leaves would be added to the structure. Lastly, that lush carpet of moss would be cut to size and placed over the top, concealing the whole thing from sight and adding a much-needed layer of insulation. Suddenly, the inside of the OP was pitch black, and the daunting realisation of our situation began to sink in. We had to stay focused throughout as day turned into night. The final details of our underground home were starting to be completed. A space for sleeping, a space for the radio, a tiny hole to watch the farmhouse through and a rear lookout position. A final glance around the forest to make sure we hadn't been spotted, and we made our way into the small entry point. Darkness and silence fell over us, and we awkwardly crawled to our starting positions, from which every two hours we would rotate. None of us were claustrophobic, but we could all feel the dense air and moist soil closing in on us, which presented a mental challenge to overcome.

Every single detail had to be recorded about the farmhouse and any goings-on in the area. For the first 24 hours, however, there was nothing, except for the departure of the Land Rover late that first evening. We continued to diligently watch the target and add to the team's panoramic sketch, which was starting to look like an architectural drawing of the landscape.

As the sun began to set on the second night of the exercise, we were exhausted, but we had to remain sharp. Suddenly, a set of headlights could be seen in the distance, moving down the track towards the farmhouse. Bennie wrote in the log book what time it was and as many details as possible as Dan reported back to HQ on the radio. They both watched as the vehicle came to a stop outside one of the small outbuildings. A figure dressed all in black exited the vehicle on the passenger side. As the sniper pair focused in on the figure, they could see a large holdall in his hand. They watched eagerly as the mysterious assailant opened the door to the barn and then crouched down, placing the bag on the ground. They were laser-focused as they watched the target and the surrounding area. The zoom on their sniper spotting scopes allowed Bennie to see the man removing rifles from the bag and placing them inside the barn. 'Positively identified target with long-barrelled weapons, mate,' said Bennie, and Dan relayed the information down the radio. The target then locked the barn doors and got back into the vehicle, and it drove away into the now pitch-black distance. It was time to swap positions, and Dan woke me up with a nudge. Waking up from a deep sleep and opening your eyes to pitch-black darkness was not a fun way to wake up. Confusion was the first challenge for each of us as we woke up, and eventually, we started to wake each other up with an explanation of where they were and what they were doing, and this mostly did the trick. Each time we swapped positions, we would be briefed by the man before on the goings on at the farmhouse or anything passed over the radio. We were also made aware of any changes to the panoramic drawing, all while in complete darkness.

The second night was cold and windy as we watched the rain move down the valley from over our heads. Our bodies were stiff and aching from enduring the weather and the fact we could barely move around inside our hide. Just as the first glimmers of daybreak arose from behind the hills, I was on lookout and had something in my sights. Peering through the tiny rabbit hole, I could make out a vehicle moving slowly down the track with no lights on, meandering conspicuously towards the farmhouse. 'Dodgy-looking vehicle here, mate,' I whispered to Gray, who was on the radio. 'Something's got to go down now, surely,' he replied as he relayed the information to HQ. I had my eyes locked onto the vehicle, which had now stopped just up the road from the barn house which held the stashed weapons. Two men exited the vehicle and walked up towards the barn, using the treeline for cover, they opened the door to the barn and entered into the dark room. Me and Gray decided to wake everyone at this point and try to get a head start on what we assumed was about to happen. The rest of the lads gradually woke up in a groggy state as me and Gray briefed them on what was happening while not taking our eyes off the target. 'Get ready, boys. You just know something is going to happen today,' said Jenks. 'They've got the weapons, and they're heading back to the vehicle now,' I whispered. The two enemy targets got into the Land Rover and pulled away slowly, again with no lights on. We all decided it best to get an early breakfast that morning and proceeded to squeeze cold sausage and beans through the ripped-off corner of our ration pouches. A method widely used to prevent the need for a spork, but the cause of painful cuts at the corner of our mouths. Once fed, we felt around the floor of our observation post to make sure that nothing was out loose or could be left behind. Our spider senses were tingling after seeing the so-called 'combat indicator' that was two armed men potentially moving towards our position.

We would be responsible for an enormous amount of kit and equipment, plus water, rations, ammunition and two weapons. The L96 sniper rifles and SA80 assault rifles would be with us at all times, which made movement somewhat difficult. However, it was made easier by rifle bags provided by Ray's ballistics expert friend Ken. Months of training and studying had all led to this point, and so had every little piece of advice given to us along the way. We were now 'thinking soldiers' capable of making life or death decisions with only ourselves to hold accountable.

Suddenly, a crack and our ears all pricked up as we held our breath. For just a few seconds, we were still. Our hands slowly felt around for our weapons as we heard more noises travelling through the woods. 'We're on, lads,' said Dan 'Here we fucking go, boys. We're getting bumped,' I said as we began to drag ourselves and our kit out of the hole. The last man's feet were still inside the hide as shots rang out through the air. Instantly, a handful of us returned fire and pushed slightly forward into cover. The call was made to ditch the heavy sniper rifles and to prepare for CQB or Close Quarters Battle. For a sniper to ditch his weapon on the battlefield is a worst-case scenario situation, but there was a protocol to it. Our weapons were to be rendered useless by smashing the scopes and removing the bolt from the rifle, taking it with us. There was no chain of command or hierarchy here. We were all equal, and no command was necessary. We all knew what we needed to do.

We took turns to throw our kit onto our backs and returned fire to suppress the advancing enemy. Once ready, we split into two fire teams and began to bound forward towards the enemy's location. Two men dressed in black could be seen running and crawling between the trees, heading directly for us, taking pot shots as they advanced. The best option for us was to neutralise the two enemy combatants and push up the steep hill until we reached the hard road at the top where we would make our extraction. The adrenaline was coursing through our bodies, and our senses were significantly heightened. We could see the two enemy figures moving quickly down the hill towards us as we split up into two fire teams. Charlie fireteam stayed central to the enemy and provided covering fire as Delta fireteam moved off to the edge of the wood. While the enemy's heads were down, Delta fireteam would advance quickly up the hill, using the more open area next to a fire break in the forest that was easier underfoot. Within a couple of minutes, we had closed in on the temporary enemy position and taken care of them. A sigh of relief was released from all of the snipers as we waited to hear 'End Ex. End Ex,' shouted from somewhere nearby, and this would all be over. Me, Dan, Gray and Bennie had made up Charlie fire team and had started to make our way through the woods to the fire break, where the rest of the lads waited. All of a sudden, we heard shots being fired from inside the forest below us. Everyone dived for cover to take a second and figure out what was going on. Two figures were running at full speed up the hill through the giant oak trees. It was a 200-metre climb for us up to our extraction road on top of the hill. We decided that the best idea would be to perform a fighting withdrawal, moving backwards up the hill. A feat that is difficult enough on flat ground, never mind up a steep slope. We would sprint in a zig-zag fashion up the hill, taking cover and returning fire every few metres. The exercise would be conducted using black rounds, and so this led to some frustration as the snipers would take shots at the advancing enemy and then them not 'play dead'. They were intent on making this as difficult as possible for us. And so the Welshmen fought our way up the hill, meter after painstaking meter, until we began to hear the sound of gravel. 'There's the fucking road, boys!' shouted Jenks. We ran as fast as we could up the hill, expending every bit of energy we had. Eventually, we reached the top, and the happiness was clear to see on all of our faces. Richie was standing on the road next to his Land Rover. We began to take our kit off, and thud after thud, it was piled on the floor. 'What the fuck are you doing?' shouted Richie. 'Get your kit on! You need to extract, you cunts!'

We all looked at each other. We weren't even surprised or phased anymore. We had become used to expecting the unexpected, and with that, we threw on our kit and began to run full pace down the road. Between us, we had all concluded that it didn't matter how far we would have to run, we were going to do it. And if the directing staff were supposed to observe our extraction, then they'd have to run the whole thing at full pace, too. Mile after mile, we ran, silent as if still in a tactical situation. We started to recognise where we were in the training area. Dixie's corner was just around the next bend. The road was at a steady incline up to the car park at Dixie's, and so we lowered our heads, widened our running strides, and powered up the hill, leaving the DS falling behind us. As we reached the car park and its stunning views of the hills, we threw down our kit and sat on it as quickly as we could. We wanted to be sat down smoking cigarettes by the time the staff arrived. A few moments later, Richie, McCormack, Osborne, Daz and Macalister reached the top of the hill and couldn't help but laugh at us all lay about as if on holiday. 'Well done fellas. Fucking good effort there. You should be proud!' shouted Richie. 'Congratulations, gents,' said McCormack 'Right, get on the buses, fellas, let's get some hot scoff.'

And with that, we jumped onto the buses and headed back to camp, the heating of the bus and the steamy windows being all it took to send us all off to sleep. After all, our extraction run had ended up being a whopping 5 miles uphill.

A sudden jolt, and we were awoken back at the parade square in camp. Without much being said, we quickly and quietly moved off to the armoury to clean our weapons. The weapons all needed a deep cleaning, which would take a few hours, all while fighting to stay awake. After the weapons had been cleaned and handed into the armoury, it was time to shower and head to the cookhouse for a decent meal. In the morning, we were met outside our rooms by Richie and Daz. 'Get a feed, gents, and then meet us outside the office for a debrief.' 'We going home today, are we then?' said Gray. 'If you get everything done quick enough, then possibly,' replied Richie. We headed off to the cook house for breakfast. As we sat at our tables chatting away and laughing about things that had happened over the past few months, the doors opened, and Daz and Osborne walked in. 'We'll get you away today, lads, don't worry. All you need to get done is clean your rooms and the shower block. We've cleaned the classrooms and office for you, and we'll take care of the armoury stuff, too,' said Daz. 'Get finished up with scoff and quickly sort the cleaning out, and you'll be away by lunchtime time, lads', said Osborne. We were made up and rushed to finish our breakfast to get off home as soon as possible.

A quick clean of the rooms and toilet blocks using aftershave and Lynx Africa-soaked socks, and we all jogged down to the office and waited for Richie and McCormack to come and debrief us, and that would be the end of the course. A quick, serious chat followed by some announcements, and we were done. 'Drive safe, fellas, and you've got the next couple of days off on leave, so get away home and return to your units in two days.' And with that, it was done. We said our goodbyes to our closest new pals, and we, one by one, jumped into our cars and headed home.

KENYA

After a well-deserved rest, all of us had returned to our units and fallen right into our battalion's training regimes. This meant that, once again, the Welshmen were split up. Stevo, Warren and Slater had been told they would be deployed in the next few weeks to Afghanistan, whereas Me, Dan, Gray, Bennie and Jenks would have a few months of extracurricular sniper training before our deployment there. We would be sent away on driving courses for various vehicles, combat medical training courses, and would also be deploying on exercise to Kenya for two months in preparation for the tour.

The courses flew by, with all of us gaining some invaluable experience and knowledge that would certainly come in handy on our upcoming tour of Afghanistan. The battalion had begun to ramp up the intensity of pre-deployment training, and the results were visible by the high standard that the troops were operating at. It was just a matter of days before the battalion would fly out to Kenya, and the newly formed Sniper Platoon were a new asset at the disposal of whoever needed us during the exercise. This meant that we would be sent out on an earlier flight to Kenya to prepare in advance, so we had a short spell at home before we left.

A few days at home had passed, and everyone headed back to camp after saying our goodbyes to our families for the next couple of months. Slowly but surely, the men turned back up in camp at our new rooms on the sniper wing of the fire support company block. As we caught up and told stories of what we had gotten up to over leave, I was quiet and sat with my head down. 'You OK, mate?' Bennie asked. 'Yeah, I'm OK, mate, just a bit of a shit few days. My Nanna died,' I said softly. The lads all began to console me, and then Dan said, 'You should go and see the boss mate and let him know. When's the funeral?' 'The day after we fly, mate,' I replied. 'Go and see the boss,' Dan demanded. I picked myself up to go and speak with the company commander and see if anything could be done. 'Hey, boss,' I said. 'My Nanna has died while I was on leave, and the funeral is the day after we're due to fly.

You think I might be able to get on a later flight?' I asked. 'Hello Ted, I'm sorry to hear that, mate. Yes, of course, I'll find out for you, but I wouldn't hold your breath.' I knew there was probably no chance, but it was worth a try. A quick phone call later, the boss was remorseful to confirm that, no, the flight could not be changed, and I would have to miss my Grandmother's funeral. It was a gut-wrenching blow, I, however, was a loyal soldier and so held my head high as I walked away down the corridor and joined the other snipers, who had begun to pack their kit ready for the flight the following day. I told the lads there would be no change and that I would be flying to Kenya with them. Pretty soon, though, I had decided I would drive back home that night to visit my Nanna at the chapel of rest and say my goodbyes before I left.

As morning broke, I made it back to camp and headed through the gates. I hastily packed my kit and joined the rest of the men on the parade square, ready and waiting for the coaches that would take us to the airport. The journey to the airport was a chance to catch up on some sleep and to reflect on my thoughts and the decision that I'd made. Before long, we had arrived at RAF Brize Norton, where we would depart for Nairobi, Kenya. The flight was fun, and the snipers all had a sense of independence as we listened to Richie's stories and plans for our further development as snipers. This was to include some 'elevated shooting through glass', which was heard so often that it became an inside joke between the lads. On the flight, Dan cast everyone's minds back to the day on the ranges in Scotland with the government suit. 'Hey lads, remember that dickhead in the suit in Scotland,' he said. 'Yeah,' we all replied. 'Well, I didn't tell anyone, but the twat asked me for a brew!' 'Did you make him one?' I replied. 'Yes!' Dan shouted. 'But I wiped my cock around the rim of the mug first!' He burst out laughing as we all fell about, crying with laughter. Over rushed the air steward to quickly ask us to keep the noise down, and we all settled back into our seats, soon to fall asleep for the remainder of the flight.

The exercise in Kenya was going to be a demanding one, especially due to its scorching temperatures and its elevation above sea level. After all, we would be training right next to the equator and not too far from Mount Kenya. The exercise would test the whole battle group and prepare them as one whole unit to deploy to Afghanistan in a matter of months. The snipers were a new asset to the battalion, and we would need to try and help our commanders use us efficiently and effectively while briefing them on our new set of skills. Richie called us a 'Force Multiplier' and even had T-shirts made for the platoon to wear with the slogan 'Force Multiplier' on the back and 'One Shot – One Kill' on the front.

We were to be split up and placed with our designated rifle companies. This was the first time we had been apart, and for the first time, we would be working in the same way that we would be out on tour in Afghanistan. Our main roles would be covert surveillance and the overwatch of foot patrols. We were joined by the rest of the troops, and acclimatisation training and environmental training began. This consisted of a few days with plenty of high-altitude running, kit issues, and safety briefs about the area, its dangers, and its wildlife. The enormous training area would be home to local tribes and villages, as well as some of the most notorious predators on earth. This place was no joke, and that became apparent just moments after landing in Nairobi.

At the back of the airport, just away from the landing strip, we were met by unmarked trucks. These trucks were to contain the troops' kit and equipment, and one truck, in particular, was to hold the weapons. 'Ted!' shouted the Sergeant Major. I made my way over to him, and I could see that I was about to be given a task to do. 'That vehicle there, mate, the one with the weapons. I need you to jump in the cab with the drivers and make sure that it all reaches our destination, OK? Stay alert, and get hold of me if anything doesn't go exactly to plan.' The drive from the airport to our destination would be a two-hour journey through the bustling back streets of Nairobi's neighbourhoods and gang lands and out through the bush. I found myself alone in a truck full of weapons, as every worst-case scenario went through my head and what I would do if any of these scenarios happened. The trip was mostly uneventful, though, on multiple occasions, people from the streets would try to jump aboard the truck in an attempt to steal whatever they could. The driver's mate, however, had a Kenyan knobkerrie, a wooden bat-shaped weapon that had a wooden tree knot at the end of it that could pack a deadly blow. As the locals would jump up to grab at anything they could get a hold of on the truck, they would soon be met by the business end of the tribal weapon. It was an eye-opening experience for me, but before long, I had safely made it to the British Army Camp at Nanyuci.

The next few days were spent sorting kit and waiting for the rest of the battalion to arrive. Acclimatisation and the related safety briefs were completed, and then it was time to move out into the bush and begin the exercise. The long drive out to the exercise location was filled with amazing things to see, hear and smell. The bustling towns and their markets were such a sight to see, made even better by the side-facing bucket seats within the huge vehicles the we had been travelling in, allowing us to sit back and take it all in. After an hour or so, the towns had started to become more like small corrugated tin villages, with dirt roads and hordes of locals lining the streets, selling cold drinks and trinkets to the troops as they passed. The children of the villages would run, cheering alongside the vehicles, and some would even try to jump aboard. It was all a new experience for us, and we enjoyed every minute of it, eager for what was to come next.

As the red dirt roads started to get bumpy, I peered off into the far distance as we started to enter the wild African bush, and I could see the magnificent rock formations so iconic to the landscape. I could see impala darting through the sparse trees and grasses and even giraffe heads bobbing around as they grazed on the higher branches. It was truly incredible, and everyone was filled with excitement as we spotted all the different animals roaming free.

After a full day of travelling, the vehicles pulled into a forward operating base deep into the bush, which was surrounded by barbed wire fences and big ditches to help protect everyone from the very real threat of lions, hyenas, elephants and everything else that goes bump in the night out there. We unloaded our kit and headed to the tented accommodation that awaited us. A quick brief about the following day's activities and we found our beds and were quickly off to sleep.

The following weeks in Kenya would consist of various training and set exercises that had been designed to be as realistic as possible, with even another regiment of troops playing the role of the enemy. The battle group scenarios would include the use of live rounds, live artillery and even helicopters, all bringing a whole new level of pre-deployment training for Afghanistan. As time went by, the exercises lengthened and increased significantly in their intensity, mainly because of the large number of dummy casualties that would be introduced throughout. One phase of the training would also include the use of laser technology, which was an eye-opening period for the troops, as they realised the importance of their training and how it might just keep them alive.

Relentless training had made for relentless fighters, and with every firefight we conducted, we grew stronger. Every single one of the men knew exactly what they needed to do at every moment, in any situation, no matter the cost. It was second nature, or maybe even by now, it had become first nature. Casualty procedures were drilled into everyone's minds, and there was good reason for it.

At this point during the war in Afghanistan, the fighting was reaching an all-time high. Heavy casualties were being taken daily, and the British death count was steadily rising. The Taliban were no fools, and their guerilla-style tactics were tried and tested for generations, defeating those who dared face them in the past. Constantly, their tactics were changing, and with every change came an update to our training. Improvised explosive devices – IEDs – were being made in all shapes and sizes, and us young troops all learnt how to get up close and personal with each of them. We learnt how to play the role of detective and the very real likelihood that we would be doing so out in Afghanistan. Conducting interviews, arrests, forensic testing, and facial recognition was soon to be a part of our job description. All this while trying to keep each other alive. The pressure was real, and the fear was real, but the troops felt neither. We were laser-focused.

Through the weeks, the snipers moved around from place to place and from company to company, occasionally spending time with Richie and catching up with each other. I had been attached to Bravo Company and was doing well, showing my new skills and putting them to the test, the same as all of the snipers had been doing. Before long, the final exercise was approaching though, and everyone was hard at work in the brutal conditions. There had been some serious injuries throughout the exercise due to the immense heat, sunstroke, heat exhaustion, and dehydration had become a very real factor. The wildlife had proven to be a formidable threat, with troops enduring attacks from snakes, scorpions, spiders, and even hyenas. The terrain had been the cause of many injuries to ankles and legs, and so had the gigantic spikes of the acacia tree been responsible for some very serious injuries, and so numbers had started to dwindle. One night, I was attached to a reconnaissance patrol heading through the night to a new location, while on top of a nearby hill, an anti-tank platoon provided overwatch through the darkness. This part of the exercise was to use blank rounds, and only senior commanders would have a single magazine of live rounds each, just in case of an emergency involving wildlife. As the patrol moved quietly through the thorny bushes and snake-riddled trees, we began to enter a section of dense jungle. The dim light of the moon cut through the canopy of leaves to illuminate just enough to see the ground. Suddenly, a strange warmth filled the air. A thick, musty smell engulfed the patrol and left us all sniffing around like a pack of dogs. Something didn't feel right, and slowly, the commanders began to swap their blank magazines for the live ones. Not all troops had night vision goggles, but those who did started to pull them down from their helmets. The heat was stifling, and the sweat poured from the men and steamed up the lenses of our goggles. All of a sudden, we heard a sound. It was a bone-trembling guttural growl that sent shivers up our spines. I quickly turned in the direction of the snarl, and there it was. A set of green eyes that watched us from behind a bush slowly started to move as another set joined them. We froze and waited for our orders over the radio. The decision was made to move away very slowly. Terrified, we slowly walked, scanning every inch of the surrounding area as we pushed towards an opening in the jungle that led to a nearby watering hole. The section, however, was being followed, and by now, the confirmation that it was a pride of lions had come over the radio. We had to stay calm, especially me, who was at the rear of the fucking pack shitting my pants. The section call sign was called over the radio, and the message 'Stop stop stop,' came echoing through the trees. Immediately, we stopped and got down on one knee. 'Yeah, gents, just stay where you are for a moment. We've got eyes on you and the lions, but there's something else. Directly in front of you through the bush is a herd of elephants who are stationary. Wait out for instructions,' said the anti-tank lads on the hill. 'Fuck me,' I thought as I tucked myself closer into the group. 'We need to fucking move, man,' I whispered to one of the blokes. With that, the radio lit up with static, and we received the order to move off quickly as the lions and elephants had both moved away. Our heart rates slowed back to normal, and leaving nothing to chance, we moved clear of the area and onto our next location.

The time spent in Kenya was full of similar incidents, some ending in bites or injuries. There was also the constant threat of the huge packs of baboons that would take any given opportunity to steal food or equipment, as experienced by the battalion Padre, who had his belt kit stolen. The local tribesmen also posed their threats and dangers. It was a common sight to be live firing at metal targets and suddenly to have a small group of locals run over to the targets, pick them up, and run off with them. Or to be mobbed by locals picking up the empty brass bullet cases ejected from the troop's weapons before they could have a chance to pick them all up. It was quite a sight to see a tribesman with a spear and shield running away with a target whilst calling someone using a mobile phone in the middle of nowhere. As our time in Kenya came to a close, we had become accustomed to interacting with the tribes and buying wooden carvings from the locals or even swapping items of clothing in exchange for carvings or trinkets. I ended up swapping a pair of trainers and a T-shirt for a hand-carved wooden plaque. The plaque was in the shape of Kenya, with my name, rank and number embossed on the front. Two days after the swap, I could hear my name being called as I lay on my bed. It was the tribesmen who had brought me my new plaque and a much-appreciated cold bottle of Coke. The carving looked amazing, and I was over the moon until I realised it had the wrong army number on it, but either way, I was happy. I chuckled to myself and thanked my new friend.

Sat back on my bed, I had time to contemplate the past few months and how demanding they had been. And then contemplating the future and what it could hold. The clear skies out in the bush allowed for the best stargazing I had ever experienced, and it encouraged me to think about everything. That, coupled with the roar of lions and the laughs of the hyenas in the distance, was to be an experience that would stay with me for a lifetime, and I was grateful for every second of my time spent in Kenya.

The following morning, it was time to leave for the final exercise, which would take place in an area called 'Archers Post', but more commonly known by the men as 'Archers Roast' because of its unbearable heat that would often sit around the 50 degrees Celsius mark. The journey would be an eight-hour torture ride in the back of a rickety old four-tonne truck with broken metal benches in the back for us to sit on. The orders came, and the troops jumped onto the vehicles and we hit the powdered dirt road, leaving a red plume behind the convoy as it moved. The first hour was OK, but we couldn't see out of the trucks this time as the canvas sheets had been pulled down and buckled shut. As we hit a main road made of concrete, the break from the rumbling through the benches was a welcome one. We all knew the drill, and quickly, everyone moved around to find a position in which to get some sleep. Sprawled all over the floors and benches, we slept in the blistering heat, occasionally awoken by locals banging in the sides of the trucks or attempting to steal kit from the back. Sleep was just as important as everything else, and we had been trained to get it whenever we could, for we may not get another chance for who knows how long.

Suddenly, the smooth tarmac turned to gravel, and we could sleep no more. The sound of the trucks rattling was deafening, and the benches were either broken in a way that pinched the back of our legs or sat on such an angle that it was just a constant stress position. 'Fuck! How long is this going to go on for!' shouted one of the lads in frustration. There was nothing to do, nothing to see, and nothing we could do about it. The toughest part of the journey was the mental battle. Two hours into the gravel road, the vehicles stopped. 'Thank fuck for that!' I shouted as one of the drivers came to the back of the truck. 'How we doing back here, gents?' he said. We knew it was pointless complaining, and so we grunted to indicate we were OK. 'Nearly there now, boys. Just six hours to go,' he said with a smile.

'Are you fucking joking!' shouted one of the lads, as the driver simply turned to walk away, replying, 'No.'

The final exercise was incredible and on a scale like we had never seen before. Hundreds of troops would mobilise on a mock village. Helicopters and artillery would bombard the village as the ground troops approached. The exercise was as real as it could get, using live rounds and explosives, the entire series of exercises ended in a crescendo of fire power that solidified the troops confidence in our abilities.

The battle group had given their all and demonstrated everything that would be used to take on the Taliban very shortly. There was a huge sense of confidence throughout the men, in ourselves and those around us, and with that, we headed away from the training area and up to our rest and recuperation week at an adventure activities resort. Here, we would have the opportunity to experience adventure activities and unwind with a cold beer. The week was full of fun and laughter as we ate BBQ food and drank beers, celebrating our endeavours and talking about our accomplishments. Bike rides with monkeys in the local national park, horse riding through villages, and white water rafting were just some of the activities on offer. The whitewater rafting, however, was reserved for those who had made themselves stand out of the crowd with their efforts. Lo and behold, the snipers were a part of the selection, and we were once again united. All except for Warren, Stevo and Slater, who had now deployed to Afghanistan. Me and Dan found ourselves in a group which consisted of men from our previous rifle company and one we held close to our hearts. Tony was the platoon sergeant and my first section commander while in basic training in Catterick, so we'd known each other for a while by then. All these other lads were me and Dan's first and closest friends in the battalion, and we had missed them all while away on our sniper cadre. Everyone was excited to go white water rafting, and after a short safety brief, we were issued our kit. A helmet, a paddle and a life jacket were given to us all as we melted in the heat hungover. Kojo, who was a part of the group, had emigrated from Ghana to Great Britain to join the British Army and to further his education. He didn't quite have the swimming skills needed to complete the rafting experience with confidence, but, with some encouragement from the lads, he boarded the blow-up raft. The river we'd be rafting down was going to prove to be no easy task. This was no Centre Parcs nonsense. This river was dangerous and not to be underestimated. Living in and around the raging river were families of hippos and crocodiles, which added to the danger element. However, eager to begin, we started to paddle while being instructed by a local rafting pro on what to do and when to do it. The course would last approximately two hours and would vary in difficulty as the rafts progressed down the river. The sun was shining, and a warm breeze drifted through the air as we looked in awe at our surroundings. It was beautiful, and for the first time in months, us young snipers felt relaxed. Every so often, the rafts would come across some white water rapids, and we would quickly jump out of our sedated state and start to paddle. Small waterfalls started to become more frequent and we traversed them with ease, while watching the baby crocs bask in the midday sun. As the water began to increase in its speed, so did its depth, which had started to make Kojo nervous. Dark humour was something that came naturally to the lads, and with that, we couldn't help but burst into fits of laughter at Kojo's fear, including the instructors. 'Guys, listen to me now, please,' said the instructor at the front of the boat, which me, Kojo and Dan sat at the back of. 'We are approaching a large waterfall in the next couple of minutes, so I just need to give you all some safety precautions.' We listened to what he had to say while Kojo hung on to every word like his life depended on it. A quick brief, and it was time to get into our brace positions in the raft and take on this waterfall. The waterfall we were about to descend was 25 feet high, with a huge lagoon at the bottom. Me and Kojo looked at each other just as the nose of our boat left the water and started to drop. 'Here we go!' I shouted, the force of the drop throwing our heads back. A couple of seconds later, the lagoon, which was now parallel to our faces, was about to swallow us whole. A huge splash, and everything fell silent. Just bubbles and blue water encased each of us as we kicked our legs and held onto that final breath we'd taken before the plunge. Eventually, we all reached the top of the water, and the adrenaline was pumping. The lads all cheered with excitement as we swam back to the rafts, which were sitting upright, waiting for us. As we all climbed aboard and scrambled to grab anything we could use to heave ourselves up with, Dan suddenly shouted, 'Where's Kojo?' I looked over on his side of the raft. 'Shit! He's not come back up!' Instantly, the lads all switched on and started to scan the area as we shouted his name. Suddenly, bubbles appeared a few metres away from the boat. Kojo's head was just about bobbing up and down in the water with his hands in the air. 'Swim, you cunt!' Shouted one of the men jokingly. 'Help me, you twats! Kojo replied. 'Oi, you better hurry up, mate. There are crocodiles behind you,' another shouted as we all fell apart laughing. 'What the fuck!' Kojo screamed, 'Fucking help me. Ted fucking help me, you bastard!' He shouted with a smile on his face. 'Fuck off', I replied as I bonked him on the head playfully with an oar. Eventually, after telling Kojo that there were no crocodiles there really, we pulled him aboard.

'OK, guys, start paddling towards the waterfall we've just come down,' shouted the instructor. 'Faster. Faster. Keep going!' he shouted even louder, battling with the noise of the waterfall that was now crashing on to our heads. 'One more big push!' he screamed. We had made our way through the stunning waterfall and into the cave that was hidden behind it like something out of a film. We floated around inside the cave in the cool, moist air which was somewhat of a break from the scorching sun. A quick paddle down river from there and the rafts were met by the vehicles to take us back to camp. Our time in Africa had come to an end, and everyone was ready to head home for a few day's leave. Taking with them memories that would last a lifetime, and life felt good.

PRE-DEPLOYMENT

Smiles covered everyone's faces as we arrived back at camp in the UK. We had proven ourselves to the battle group, and now the battalion knew what we were capable of, and it changed a lot. The next few months would be a chance for us to sharpen our shooting skills and to also work with our companies and integrate with their training regimes ready for deployment.

Time at home was just what we needed before our final push to deployment, and everyone was looking forward to reuniting with their families. The sun was out, and the beer gardens were full. Occasionally checking in on each other and arranging to meet up, the snipers would talk on the phone, especially me and Dan, who lived in the same village. One afternoon, while catching up with my local mates, my phone rang, and Dan's name lit up on the screen. 'Two seconds, lads. I just need to get this,' I said.

'Hi, mate,' excited that Dan might come out for a drink with me that day. 'Hi, mate,' Dan replied quietly. 'Have you seen the news today?' he asked. 'No mate, why? I replied in a concerned tone. 'It's Stevo, mate.' The world stopped moving for a second as I spoke softly. 'Fuck. No mate. What happened?' I walked away from my group of friends to conceal the conversation. 'He's dead, mate. He's fucking dead. He got hit by an IED, and he's gone.' For just a second, I couldn't believe what I was hearing. 'No way. There must be some kind of mistake here,' I said to Dan as both of our voices trembled. 'Go home and put on the news mate. Look, I have to go, OK, but I'll call you later.' 'Yeah, OK, mate,' I replied as I hung up the phone. 'Hey, boys. Something happened, and I need to shoot off home. I'll call you all later, OK.' And with that, I ran home as fast as I could. As I reached my parents' home, I slowed to a walk and caught my breath. Nothing seemed to feel like it was real. And I certainly didn't want to worry my mum and dad. So I stopped on the driveway to smoke a cigarette and calm my nerves. I slowly opened the front door to see my parents both sitting on the sofa, my mum with tears in her eyes that she did her best to hide. Slowly,

I walked towards the doorway of the living room, and as I did, I caught a glimpse of the TV. There he was. His picture filled the entire screen as newsreaders told the brief story of what had happened. It was Stevo. And he was gone. I started to shake as the tears bubbled up from inside me that I'd held in so well. The tears fell from my eyes, and my bottom lip quivered as my fists clenched. So quickly, the sadness turned into rage as I pounded my knuckles against the wall. 'I'm going to make them pay for this,' I said, shaking my head in disbelief.

All of a sudden, things had changed, and the reality I was about to face came smashing me in the face. There was a very realistic chance that I could be killed too, but no matter what, I vowed to myself that I would keep those realities away from my parents as best as I could. This was something that most of the men did; it was for self-preservation. To do this job and to stay alive, we had to become callous and shut down our feelings. The added stress of worrying about people back home could potentially be just enough to distract us at the wrong time. The snipers all called around each other that day and made sure everyone was OK as we planned our attendance at Stevo's funeral.

Days went by, and the morning came. We ironed our uniforms and polished our medals before driving to our brother's home town. A sea of people gathered around the church as soldiers lined the roads, and those lucky enough made their way into the rows of wooden benches inside the church. TV cameras and News teams parted as we made our way up to the church and entered through the giant wooden doors. We sat in silence with our heads held high as the funeral service proceeded and the obituaries were read aloud through broken voices. The hymns sounded as if they were being sung by an all-male choir as the Welsh troops gave their friend the send-off he deserved by singing at the top of our voices. It was a strange moment for us, almost as if able to glimpse into what could be in our own futures, as daunting as that was true. The wolf pack had lost one of their own and, with it, a little piece of ourselves. Celebrations of Stevo's life continued through the night as a music festival was held at the family farm in his honour, but the snipers quietly left our beloved friend with a quiet goodbye.

The weeks went by back at camp as training continued to escalate. Physical tests had become designed to push every man to their limits and to be able to perform effectively in that state for quite some time and even beyond. One day, Richie gathered us all together and said, 'Right, lads, I'm taking you out of your rifle companies for a couple of weeks, and we're going shooting. We are going to send so many rounds down that range that it will become impossible for you to miss.' This came as a welcome surprise to us as the level of training at the company level had now become monotonous, when we should be putting that time to good use and continuing to push ourselves further than before. The snipers packed our bags and jumped onto our faithful companions, the minibuses, and headed off to the shooting ranges for the next couple of weeks.

Day after day, we lay behind our weapons from dawn till dusk, firing round after round at the targets and hitting them with ease every time. We knew our weapons every detail by extensively testing each of our rifles repeatedly. We were at the top of our game, and at the end of our time on the ranges, the smiles had returned to our faces, and our confidence was high, we all knew just how good we had become. We returned to our battalion after firing thousands of rounds on those ranges and rejoined our rifle companies, who had begun to wind down for pre-deployment leave. Huge cardboard boxes were issued to us all, two each. The first was for any military kit that would not be going with us to Afghanistan, and the second was for any civilian items, which would be divided into 'for the lads' and 'for the family' sections if we were killed. Along with packing our boxes, we had to complete various forms, which included our wills. The standard response was, 'Everything goes to my parents, and put a grand behind the bar for the funeral'. Song choices had to be made for our funerals, and this sparked up a few laughs at people's comical choices, which lightened the morbid mood in the room. The sound of packaging tape and thuds echoed through the halls as we finished up and began to stack our boxes by our beds. Columns of brown boxes housed the lives of hundreds of young men, their fates yet undecided.

The lights went off as the snipers made our way out of the building and over to the car park. A strange feeling was hanging over us, which would phase in and out of our minds over the next weeks' leave. I hit the road and was welcomed home by an early Christmas dinner with my family. It was a wonderful moment, but as time went on, the fact that I was going to war again was present in everyone's mind. I avoided the subject as much as I could. However, I had made some video messages for my family to watch on Christmas morning, and on announcing what I'd done, the tears began to fall. My mum couldn't keep it in any longer, and with good reason. She had met lots of the army boys and not only worried about her son but his friends too. She knew other mothers whose sons would be deploying with me to Afghanistan, and that brought a strange sense of comfort to them all. I was more worried about my mum while I was away than I ever was about myself, whereas my dad had served in the military himself and had experienced the Falklands War. It helped that he understood the feelings I had and that, more importantly, he could listen to anything I had to say.

It seemed like only a blink of an eye when the troops' deployment leave came to an end, and one by one; the snipers returned to camp. Most were dropped off by parents or partners, and I watched the heart-wrenching event unfold through the steamed-up windows of my father's car as we slowly pulled up into the car park next to the enormous barbed wire guardroom gates. It was a very heavy moment for everyone, with children crying hysterically as they refused to let go of their father's legs and the howling cries of wives about to spend the next six months alone. I swiftly opened the car boot of my dad's car and took out my bags, taking a deep breath in private before my family got out of the car. We embraced and said our goodbyes, fighting back the tears while I became callous. 'I love you guys,' I said as I slowly turned and walked towards the dimly lit guardroom and walked off into the darkness of the barracks. I could hear the faint sobbing of my mother as I walked away, and at that very moment, I pulled down the veil. The person I had to be in order to stay alive was there now, and there was no looking back, I couldn't. Happiness was left at that dimly lit guardroom gate, and it would be over a decade until I would be reunited with happiness, following, well . . . what was to come. I was nervous but calm. I was ready to fight but hesitant to. I'd trained harder than ever before, but nothing could have prepared me for what was to come next.

AFGHANISTAN

Two weeks before Christmas, the coaches were lined up on the parade square, ready and waiting for the battalion of men to board as the snow softly fell. Kit checks were complete, and the troops began to move. Quietly yet with a sense of urgency, we boarded the coaches and sat in our seats. Nobody spoke during the drive, with most using the time to just get in some sleep. As the coaches neared RAF Brize Norton, the men began to stir as whispers and deep breaths made their way towards the back of the bus. The lads who'd been to Afghanistan before, well, we knew what to expect. We knew the devastation that would meet us at the other end of this flight, but we kept it hidden like a secret to be learned by the rest of the lads in due time. The flight would leave the UK and land in Cyprus, which is where we would board a different aircraft for our final flight into Afghanistan.

The flight to Cyprus was a snooze fest, but not a wink of sleep was to be had on that flight into Afghanistan, and before long, the captain came over the speakers, calmly informing us that we were now over Afghan airspace and that they would be switching over to tactical flight procedures imminently. The guy who's first time it was looked around, unaware of what this meant. 'Helmets and body armour on, get ready!' was shouted down the plane from front to back as we a quickly stowed away our belongings and prepared ourselves.

As the seat belt signs above our heads illuminated the helmets of the Welshmen, all of the lighting inside the aircraft suddenly went to blackout, and then they all turned red. I took a deep breath, and the plane suddenly began to drop out of the sky, and my stomach flew up into my chest. The pilot was conducting a tactical drop, and until we were under radar detection range, we would be in a dead engine drop. Our stomachs, by now, felt like they were in the back of our throats as troops gripped tightly to the armrests, hoping that everything was under control and that this would soon be over.

The engines started back up, and we began our approach to Kandahar Air Base just as orders began to be distributed out between the troops and RAF aircrew. The plane landed safely, and swiftly we disembarked the mostly civilian-looking aircraft to collect our bags and head through security. The heat was an astonishing blast to the face, and the air had a sort of dense feel, accompanied by a strange smell that could only be described as mouldy dust. The next few long hours would consist of mostly administration and waiting around while paperwork and checks were completed on every single person arriving in the country. Most spent the time reading or watching a tiny TV while eating soggy sandwiches out of brown paper bags.

Checks were eventually complete, and we collected our gear and swiftly, we made our way through the security gates and back out into the sweltering heat of the airstrip. Our next taxi through the air would be the real deal. The engines of the aircraft took the men's breath away with its intense streams of fiery hot air as we made our way up to the tailgate at the back end of the plane and finally into the side-facing military-style bucket seating. As the last of the troops took their seats, a few crates of supplies were loaded into the centre of the craft, and the tailgate went up. Everything was cast into a red darkness as the tactical lighting lit up our faces.

'OK, gents, only a short flight, and we'll be landing you at Camp Bastion,' said one of the RAF crew, and he continued to brief the troops as we all strapped ourselves in. 'And finally, is it anyone's birthday today?' The crewman called out. I threw up my hands and shouted, 'Yes. Me!' excitedly. 'OK mate, up you come,' said one of the pilots who was standing in the doorway. I unbuckled my seat straps and made my way to the front of the aircraft and through into the cockpit area. 'That's your seat tonight, right there, mate,' said the other pilot, who was already in position at the front left-hand seat conducting his final checks. I placed myself in the rear centre seat that was sat only slightly behind the two pilots' seats. In front of me was a galaxy of red, green and orange buttons and levers. At the epicentre of the confusion was a huge-handled lever that turned out to be the throttle. Some quick radio chatter, and the first pilot turned to me. 'OK mate, your turn. Just slowly push that bad boy forward, and we'll get our asses out of here.' It wasn't actually my birthday, and so I was made up with the outcome of my little white lie. 'Let's fucking do this!' I shouted, and the plane began to pull away. Faster and faster down the runway we went as I gradually pushed the throttle forward. The aircraft reached optimum speed, and the pilots both kicked into action as they sent the plane up into the night sky. It was amazing, and just for a moment, there was an overwhelming sense of calm as I watched the stars come into sight. Moments later, the bubble had been well and truly burst as I peered out of the front window at the burning buildings below, which snapped me right back to reality. I was back in Afghanistan, and the war I had left behind only a year earlier was still raging on, but this time it was different. This time, I was filled with vengeance.

The short flight soon came to an end, and we landed at Camp Bastion, our base of operations for the majority of the next six months. A hot dust bowl in the middle of the desert that was big enough to be seen from space would house us for the next two weeks while we conducted our in-theatre training on the latest techniques and were briefed on the latest goings on in Helmand Province. The base held multiple nationalities of soldiers, and they would often deploy on coalition operations together. Everything we needed was there, from shops and an internet connection to several fast food outlets made out of shipping containers. The food in the UK cookhouse was pretty good, and it was plentiful, which helped a lot with morale, but it would soon become only a distant memory.

The days went by of conducting fitness training and weapon training. The snipers zeroed in our scopes and prepared our weapons for war. Some training continued through the night for the troops using various vehicles, and we needed to test our driving at night. The snipers did the same with our night sights, which also had infrared and thermal capabilities. The latest in medical and tactical training was tested repeatedly until every man was as capable as the next in multiple fields.

We were to start the tour as a part of the battalion Mobile Reconnaissance Force – MRF – mounted on Jackal lightweight vehicles, and tasked with heading deep into the desert to probe outlying enemy positions and training grounds. The MRF would consist of eighteen vehicles, each armed with a General Purpose Machine Gun, a light machine gun, and either a fifty-calibre machine gun or a grenade machine gun. All of that firepower, plus personal weapons, anti-tank missiles and the snipers, meant that this was not an outfit to be messed with and if needed, we could rain down hellfire on our enemy. The team would spend our days overlooking or patrolling through small villages. Ghost towns that sometimes housed as little as single-digit populations would engulf us with their towering 15-foot-high walls, which certainly left us feeling vulnerable a lot of the time. By sundown, we would head far out into the desert and camp up for the night until doing the same again the following day. The extremes in temperature difference from day to night became somewhat of a battle in itself, with temperatures ranging from 30 degrees Celsius to 15 below zero on the same day. We went from village to village, and as we progressed, we grew in our confidence and our abilities, all while navigating the small arms firefights we got into, which came with the Taliban outposts we found.

Our first operation soon came to a close, and the MRF headed back to Camp Bastion, where we would replenish what we needed and gear up for the next job, which would be a coalition operation with the Estonian army. The MRF moved with our Jackal vehicles out to the next location after a quick refit and rest. A sparsely populated area that was made up mostly of wet and muddy farmland and huge compounds with the occasional treeline and ditch running alongside the fields. The rocky terrain made for a bumpy journey to the forward operating base, which was run by the Estonians but also home to a large group of Afghan Army soldiers.

As years went by in the Afghan war, there had been a noticeable change, which meant that British soldiers now played a different role. The days of kicking in doors and throwing grenades were coming to an end, and now the troops were playing almost the role of a police officer or a detective. Questioning and arresting the Taliban or holding conferences with local tribesmen while checking fingerprints and testing for gunpowder residue had become a common occurrence for the men. This was conducted while also fighting and defending these areas from the Taliban at the same time as training the Afghan Army for them to one day take over and be able to be independent. This, however, was no easy task for the British troops. Often unwilling to cooperate or high on opium, the Afghan soldiers were, more often than not, no help during a firefight or the various other jobs that had to be done.

As the MRF slowly pulled into the muddy FOB, we could see the tented accommodation, a small cookhouse tent, and some more accommodation tents at the rear of the base. The Estonians and the MRF would be camped up next to each other, while the Afghan Army had the bottom rows of tents to themselves. It didn't take long for us and the Estonians to start getting to know each other while we sat around a fire barrel to keep warm. The snipers would all be working closely together in the area, and we began to talk weapons and tactics with each other. During their conversation, the Estonians passed on the latest Taliban goings-on in the area to us and sneakily told us about the sauna. 'What fucking sauna?' I said. 'That small tent over there,' pointed out one of the Estonian snipers. 'No fucking way!' said Gray, laughing in amazement. The Estonians went on to tell us boys about how they made a sauna tent everywhere they went and how it was a big part of their setups and culture.

The conversation continued and then suddenly turned from a light-hearted chat to a quiet word of advice. The Estonians had been there with the Afghan soldiers for quite some time, and over that time, they had overheard and witnessed some questionable things. They disclosed that there had been some rumours and some allegations between the Afghan soldiers. At this time during the war, there had been several incidents involving Afghan soldiers or policemen, who had been Taliban insurgents masquerading as uniformed officers. Whispers and rumours spread around the base over the next few days, and everyone was clearly on edge. Suddenly, an almighty fight broke out in the Afghan accommodation tents. They had found the rat, and he was being dragged around the floor by the Afghan soldiers as they kicked and punched the infiltrator. As the commotion moved further away towards the main gate, it brought a small sense of relief to the MRF lads as we prepared our kit for our imminent patrol. At least we could rest slightly easier knowing the rat had been captured. As for what would happen to him, well, that was none of our concern.

The first patrol would be on foot, leaving a small rear party to look after the vehicles and anything else left behind at the base. The patrol was long but uneventful, as was the case for most patrols in the area. However, our presence was still much needed as a show of force, if nothing else, and soon we would expand our area of operations, flushing out the Taliban from their hiding places and forcing them to face the consequences of their actions.

The weather was cold and wet most days, but this didn't bother us British troops too much. It was what we were used to, but for the Taliban, that was not the case. The fighting would significantly slow down during the colder months but would soon pick up as the weather began to improve. Time went by, and with it came another move for the MRF. This time, we would be joined by some other troops from our battalion, and we would be heading towards the edge of the secured area in the hope of pushing back the Taliban towards an area known as the green zone. The area which the great Helmand River would traverse and with it bringing dense vegetation and lots of activity.

After the regroup, the troops advanced towards the suspected positions. The route would be a tricky one and would include thick vegetation and some wall climbing to ensure a covert approach. Men had telescopic ladders attached to their backs, secured and ready for them to be able to simply kneel at a wall while the person behind extended the ladder for everyone to run up. It was a long, difficult insertion, with the heat now reaching that of a British summer, but soon enough, we reached the compound we would call home for a few days. A team cleared the compound, and then the various groups were briefed by their commanders and sentry duties were allocated. The lads began to check each of the rooms of the compound until it was deemed safe. These searches and checks would often result in finding rooms filled with cannabis buds, oil drums full of heroin, bomb-making materials or weapons. This one in particular. Well, this one had a room filled to the ceiling with cannabis that had been harvested from the surrounding miles of fields. On instructions to stay away from the room, we started to set up in our allocated sleeping quarters.

Once everyone was settled in, a small section of men headed out to establish our arrival to the locals. These types of patrols were usually a way of drawing out Taliban fighters by allowing them to take a free shot, to some extent. The Taliban were extremely hard to spot, and a lot of soldiers would never lay eyes on them. You see, the Taliban knew these areas like the back of their hand, and they had made strategic changes to buildings to aid them in being able to fire a few shots off and then disappear into the labyrinth of small holes and tunnels that lead away from the villages. Reactions had to be lightning-fast. Otherwise, there was no way of catching them.

Ten minutes into the patrol leaving the new base, the all too familiar 'crack, zip' sound was heard flying through the air. 'Crack, zip, thud', went the Taliban rounds as they flew towards the compound and then suddenly towards the men out on patrol. We scrambled out of our rooms and snatched our weapons from the ground. Quickly between us, we organised who was going where and who was doing what. We began to climb boxes and huge sacks of rice to reach the top of the compound walls. Some of the lads on stag had started to return fire already. 'Where's it coming from?' shouted Bennie. 'Over that direction somewhere!' one of the lads shouted back. We scanned the area surrounding us, having every angle covered, and then all fell quiet. It was a shoot-and-scoot, and the Taliban had immediately left the area and were more than likely going to report to their commanders.

AND THEN THERE WERE FOUR

After a few weeks, the smaller villages were done with, and the Taliban had been pushed back, back to the green zone. The snipers were then split up and began to be posted out to various rifle companies or to whoever needed us. As we went our separate ways, Dan had been tasked to go out on a job with one of the rifle companies. They were to leave Bastion before first light and move onto a Taliban stronghold via Chinook helicopter, where they would flush out the enemy and then secure the area.

The day started in cold, wet darkness as Dan carried his kit over to the airstrip where the helicopters would be waiting, everyone around him quiet with anticipation. Those few minutes before boarding a flight were mostly calm, and then as the troops load into the choppers. Well, that's when the adrenaline starts to kick in. Dan boarded the dimly-lit helicopter and sat, ready to take on what was about to come. A short flight through the night sky and they would arrive at their target location. Split into two helicopters, the company approached their position while flying low to remain undetected for as long as possible. As they began their descent, the first Chinook touched down in an open field. It was soaking wet, and the mud was several feet deep. The first chopper got bogged down in the thick mud as it attempted to land. Instantly, the second chopper pulled away and circled back around, leaving space for the grounded Chinook to eventually manoeuvre itself free.

The second helicopter approached the ground and hovered over the thick mud; its tail pointed slightly upwards as the tailgate began to lower. 'Standby, men! Go, go, go!' shouted the aircrew. Without hesitation, the men, ready in a row, ran towards the back of the aircraft, and they jumped. Dan, as a sniper, was carrying a considerably heavier amount of kit than most troops, and as he leapt from the back of the Chinook into total darkness, he thought his best chance of landing safely would be to land double-footed. His boots sank deep into the freezing mud, and his 100-plus pounds of kit threw him violently to the floor, resulting in both of his knees being crushed into rocks that littered the mud below him. He was in agony as he turned to look behind him at the chaos that had unfolded. Men were falling to the ground from the helicopter, which, on the angle it was, had made for a much bigger drop than they had anticipated, and the guys jumping had no idea what they were jumping into. Several men suffered broken bones as they piled on top of each other underneath the hovering aircraft.

Suddenly, as Dan watched, he began to see tracer rounds flying through the air towards the helicopters, the sound of the rounds just barely audible over the giant engines of the helicopters. The Taliban had opened fire at them using a Dushka anti-aircraft gun. There was no time to lose, and Dan began to crawl his way to the edge of the muddy field and into cover, his knees screaming with pain with every move he made. The Chinooks had to take off, and it had to be now, otherwise they could be in very serious trouble. Dan looked on as he just hoped that none of the anti-aircraft rounds would hit and possibly blow up one of the choppers that hovered above his head. With haste, however, the choppers pulled up and away into the night sky, leaving a mass of casualties in the mud that needed attention. There was no other choice, and so the troops spread out, encircling the injured lads and providing them with some security. This was not a long-term plan, however, and the helicopters had to return to evacuate the injured. Soon enough, the helicopters appeared out of the darkness. Bringing relief to the ground troops, but as soon as they came, they had to leave again due to the heavy machine gun fire heading straight in their direction. They pulled away again as the troops on the ground took cover and tried to suppress the enemy fire. Suddenly, the Chinooks appeared again. However, this time, it was a distraction tactic. They planned to draw the fire of the Taliban, and as they did so, an Apache attack helicopter approached from low in the distance. They had locked on to the enemy position and let loose their Hellfire missiles. The missiles soared through the black sky and landed directly on top of the anti-aircraft gun, obliterating the entire area. Compounds were left nothing but dust, and everything fell quiet.

The Chinooks had left, and the Apache was just about to leave as the Black Hawk medical evacuation teams arrived and safely evacuated the casualties. Dan, however, stayed behind, and for the next two weeks, he patrolled and fought in the area, all while the injuries he sustained to his knees continued to worsen. At the end of the operation, he returned to Camp Bastion, and on his arrival, he was sent to the medical centre for some treatment and pain medication. It turned out the injuries he had sustained from leaping out of the hovering aircraft had done serious damage to his knees, and there was no other choice but for him to return to the UK for rehabilitation. Concurrent with this operation, the other snipers had been sent off on various other jobs of their own and were unaware of what had happened to Dan.

The snipers would be working without spotters on the tour and would be spread thin throughout the battalions, hundreds of men. Me, Bennie and Gray had been attached to a small group out patrolling a hot location. At this point in the war, enemy snipers had become a big issue. There had also been reports of foreign fighters or, more like, foreign snipers, in particular, being paid to join the Taliban fight against coalition troops. Many British troops had already been shot by these enemy snipers, and it was something that was at the forefront of all our minds. We had flown into an area that resembled a no man's land depicted in a war movie. Large empty fields and bombed-out buildings surrounded the area, while small settlements of locals remained on the outskirts of the devastated land. After a couple of small patrols around the area, the locals became very welcoming to us and even made us food and fresh bread as we patrolled past their houses. It reminded us of our reasons for being there. These people needed to be helped, and us Welshmen certainly intended to do everything in our power to help them.

One morning, we woke early for a patrol that would take us further away from the base than before, and today, we would be joined by an Afghan Special Forces unit. We threw our kit onto our backs and began the patrol that would last all day, carrying with us everything we may need. The snipers had split ourselves up into the front, centre, and rear of the patrol so that we had the best coverage of the surrounding area. There was something in the air that day, and we could feel imminent danger lurking around every corner. The streets were empty, the villagers all hidden away inside their locked compounds. Things like this were called a combat indicator, and the lads were all like a coiled spring, just waiting for it to kick off. The roads were only short in the village, with 15-foot walls and giant metal doors, the compounds that lined the roads could be hiding anything.

Every corner was taken with care as we scanned every hole in the wall or potential rooftop position for enemy fighters. After miles of tense patrolling, the buildings began to spread out, and we could soon see open fields coming up ahead of us. The team slowly made our way towards the opening in the buildings and took cover in a deep irrigation ditch. A gravel road went through the centre of the fields to our front and led to another village. The ditches at the side of the road were plush with tall green reeds, which we used to conceal ourselves. The British troops had taken up position in the western ditch, while the Afghan forces had taken up their position in the eastern ditch. We then both simultaneously made our way up the ditches, heading towards the next village, scanning the surrounding fields and buildings eagerly. After just a short while of us moving forward down the 1,000-metre-long road, the interpreter for the British troops told us that something was wrong.

He continued to tell us that he was tuned in to the Taliban's radio frequency, and he could hear what they were saying. Up ahead, the fields were nothing but thick, heavy, wet mud. The Taliban planned to wait for us to get midway through the field, get nice and stuck in the mud, and then they would open fire on us. At this point, we had no idea where the Taliban were hiding, and that was a concern. Andy was in command of our team and soon tasked us snipers with pushing forward and locating the enemy. He'd been working with us from the start of the tour and earlier in pre-deployment training and was even the commander on my vehicle in the MRF. He knew each of the snipers well, and the lads trusted him, and just as importantly, we liked him.

We wasted no time and began to move a little forward from the pack to gain a vantage point. The reeds were too high, and we couldn't get the view we needed without compromising our positions. As we waited for the rest of the team to catch up to us, we took position sat hidden low in the reeds. The plan was made to enter the muddy field and advance into battle, knowing that it would end in a firefight, but also giving the men the advantage of being able to properly look at the surrounding area and potentially the enemy position.

The sun was high in the sky as the British troops made our way into the knee-deep muddy field. Every step was made more difficult by the mud sticking to our boots and weighing us down. Lucky for us, we wouldn't have to wait that long for the Taliban to open fire on us, which felt like a bit of a silver lining to be honest. Immediately, we returned fire and began to conduct a fighting withdrawal back into the reeds as we tried to spot the enemy. Just as the men began to move backwards, we could see movement on the road next to us. The Afghan Special Forces lads had decided that they would all just leg it up the road and see what awaited them at the end. Some of the Welshmen laid down suppressing fire to support the Afghan soldiers on their assault, and then we made our way back into the reeds to take cover. The snipers took position higher up on the bank to get a better view, although we instantly felt the danger we were in. The enemy fire was coming from the north, in the direction the road was heading. A huge explosion went off and the Afghan forces had breached the door of the compound where the fire was coming from, followed swiftly by some bursts of automatic fire and then silence. The Afghan soldiers had taken the enemy position in the distance, and us snipers then began to scan the area for enemy depth positions. As we did so, another position opened fire. It was coming from the group of buildings and trees to the west of our position. This was a classic Taliban tactic to have multiple positions fire at different times, and the lads knew that we could be under threat of being surrounded if we didn't act quickly.

The bullets whistled as they flew just inches from the our heads. The troops returned fire in the general direction and an anti-tank missile was fired towards the building closest to where some of the enemy fire was coming from. Everyone was returning fire as I slowly and methodically searched the buildings with my scope. Rounds were landing all around me, but I had to stay calm and do what I was there to do, what I was trained to do. I spotted something moving near a gap in the wall. It looked like a shadow being cast by someone hiding behind the 6-foot wall to the front of a building that looked like it was a school. Target indications were shouted out amongst the men trying to pin down the enemy as the snipers began to fire. We had all seen the movement that was behind the wall and then a barrel. The muzzle of an AK-47 popped around the wall, and the snipers fired simultaneously. We cocked the bolts of our weapons and chambered our next rounds. We watched the area as an order of 'cease fire' was yelled down the line. The men waited and watched. The snipers checked every inch of the buildings and alleyways in the area to see any retreating enemy, but we saw nothing. The enemy fighter was down, and we slowly made our way back down into the ditch and made our way back towards base. The setting sun bathed the landscape in a dark orange glow that was like something out of this world watching over the troops. Although exhausted, we had to stay alert as the threat of another attack loomed over our heads. As the adrenaline left our bodies and morale grew high, we reached our temporary home, ate and then slept like bears.

THE ENEMY SNIPER

'Lads, wake up. You're needed,' said a voice quietly in the darkness. 'Boys, grab your kit and meet us outside.' Me, Gray and Bennie rubbed our eyes and quickly got our kit on, then headed outside of the hangar where we had been set up for the night. Our cot beds were still warm as we met with a small group that was waiting outside the hangar. One of the guys in the group was Adi. A Fijian legend from the battalion who was a sharpshooter on the tour and had been picked to join the impromptu operation with his L96 sniper rifle. 'Anyone know what the fuck this is about?' said one of the blokes.

A small section of British troops had been pinned down for weeks in a compound not too far away from our location. They had been pinned down by an enemy sniper and had taken heavy casualties while struggling to get a resupply of food, water and ammunition. Our small task force had been contacted over the radio and ordered to establish face-to-face contact with the isolated British troops and, where possible, engage with the enemy in the area.

As morning broke, the warm glow of the sun lit up the buildings and trees en route to the target area. Afghanistan was a beautiful country, and it held scenery that would stay with me forever, but today was not a day to be distracted by the scenery. The insertion to the target area would be around 8 miles long. Eight miles of constant awareness and the pressure of imminent attack made for a tiresome start to the day. As the team got closer to the area where the British troops were pinned down, the landscape began to change. The fields were filled with debris and old vehicles. Most of the buildings were blown to pieces or covered in bullet holes. This had been the site of some very intense fighting. We moved slowly forwards. Every small hole in a wall could be a 'murder hole'. A murder hole was used by the Taliban to simply stick the barrel of their weapon through and open fire at the troops while in excellent cover themselves. The team contacted the stranded troops over the radio, and they prepared to open the gates and let us in. The final move in was a swift one.

In through the gates, and one by one, the Welshmen moved into the compound. The soldiers there looked exhausted but relieved as we met in the middle of the courtyard to make our plan. All around us stood broken-looking men who had been surviving on minimal rations and had lost some of their friends by the look in their eyes. Their sheer will to continue was inspiring to the Welsh snipers, and we wanted to help. In command of the small team were Chris and Tony. Two of the best commanders that the battalion had to offer. Together with the snipers, we devised a plan to observe the area to the front of the compound where we had been briefed that the enemy sniper fire was coming from, while the rest of the troops shared out their rations, water and ammunition with the depleted section of stranded troops, and then began to make their plan to defend the compound.

Me and Gray were to climb up to the tower position in the south-west corner of the compound, while Bennie and Adi climbed up to the second tower position in the north-west corner. We made our way over to the abandoned towers and started to climb the wooden ladders up to the sand-filled hessian baskets. A thick wire cubic cage frame that was lined with hessian material and filled with sand and gravel that measured approximately two metres square. On top of these, we would have smaller sandbags to help with cover. As Gray and myself reached the top of the ladder, we both sneakily peered over the top of the sandbags to look at the ground in front of us. Bennie and Adi did the same in their position, and what we all saw looked like it was from a scene in an old WW2 sniper movie. Collapsed buildings and huge craters from bombs that had been dropped were strewn all over the landscape, and small patches of vegetation had started to grow amongst the older piles of debris. It made for an enemy sniper's heaven and also made for our nightmare. I dropped my head down below the sandbags and started to think about what I could do.

Seconds later, a huge crack flew through the air, and Gray dived for cover, as did me, Bennie and Adi. The enemy sniper that had terrorised the area had spotted us in just a few seconds and taken a shot at Gray's head, missing it by inches. We all looked around at each other, and Chris and Tony looked up at us with a worried look from the ground. Slowly, we prepared ourselves to take another look and hopefully be able to spot the enemy sniper in his hide. I popped my head up, and another shot rang out through the air. It sounded different to anything else that had been fired at us in the past. It sounded powerful, and this guy was getting closer with his shots, again only missing my head by inches. The game was on, and a helmet was even lifted above the wall on a stick to attract the sniper fire to allow us to observe the area as best as we could. At this point, we hadn't even managed to place our weapons onto the sandbags, let alone spot the enemy sniper and do the relevant calculations needed to neutralise him.

Another deafening shot rang out. 'Fuck!' shouted Bennie at the top of his lungs. For just a split second, everyone listened for screams of pain. Luckily, nobody had been hit. However, Bennie and Adi had come way too close for comfort. 'Fuck this, Adi, let's get down from here before we get shot, shall we,' said Bennie. The enemy sniper had fired into their hessian basket defence wall. The round was so powerful that it had flown straight through the gravel wall, through a container of ammunition, through a wooden railway sleeper, and off into the distance. Whatever that weapon was that he was using, it was extremely powerful and not to be underestimated. Not only that, but we knew that this guy knew what he was doing, and the chances of him missing again were slim. There was no other option; we had to move. We climbed down from our towers as hopeless faces looked back up at us. A sight that would stick with me for many years to come. Tony and Chris came up with a plan to move over to the next compound, which would provide us with a better angle and a potential shot at the now presumed foreign rebel hired gun.

Slowly, we threw on our kit and took a welcome sip of water. We all lined up next to a small blue door at the side of the compound, now opposite where we had initially entered. Looking into the eyes of each other and shouting, 'Come on, boys!' The Welshmen prepared each other for what we were about to do, and each of us shared a moment in time that not many people could even imagine. We were going to attempt to sprint across the 100-metre-long gap between that blue door and the red door of the next compound. Individually, we would run for our life, with no covering fire and no smoke grenades to mask our movements, as this would attract the eye of the enemy sniper and give away our position. Cigarettes were passed down the line of men as if awaiting the gallows. Even the men who didn't smoke did at that moment.

In a situation like that, there is a very particular place that you have to go to within your mind. It is a place where you must be willing to die but be positive that you won't. A place where emotions no longer exist. A place where you can almost feel every single detail imaginable being flooded into your consciousness at millisecond interludes. While the entire world seems to appear slowed down and almost unreal, like an out-of-body experience, you seem to float through the moment in a giddy state.

I moved slowly up the line as the first few men dashed out of the doorway. Smoking the last of my cigarette quickly, I readied myself.

I braced behind the doorway, all my weight on my front left leg. Ready, I took a deep breath into my soul. There seemed to be a rapidly changing feeling in the air of when was good to run and when was not a good time. The ebb and flow of life and death were floating around the atmosphere like a Valkyrie overwatching the battlefield, ready to guide home the souls of the lost. 'Now!' I thought, and I ran for my life as rounds flew around me. Zig-zagged my way towards the red door, just as I had done so many times before. Varying speeds and randomising my movements, I burst through the red door of the next compound, where the guys who had already dashed had started to clear the rooms. The last of the Welshmen made it across the near-death run and into the new compound walls. Just as the last man came bursting through the door, Tony and Chris were busy on the radio. The lads started to overhear their conversation and heard something about there being air assets in the area, and they might be heading our way.

All of a sudden, we heard, 'Yeah, Roger, that Witchcraft42. Right, lads, get the fuck down. There are two Apaches on their way to us flying low.' There was a feeling of instant relief throughout the troops, but also a feeling of discontent held between the snipers, who had wanted to get this guy ourselves. 'Boom!' Explosion after explosion, followed by howling machine-gun fire billowing down from the two heavily-armed attack helicopters which were now overhead. Within a few moments, the entire area had been completely flattened, and clouds of dust filled the air. Whoever that enemy sniper was, he certainly wasn't there anymore.

A short while later, the task force made our way back to the FOB and reunited with the other troops who'd been out patrolling elsewhere that day. The men had no idea, but we would be extracting the very next day and sharing a chopper with the now safe and sound cut-off British troops. Happy days. We spent the night before our flight passing out exhausted on the floor of an old government building's front gardens. That night, the locals showed their gratitude by coming in numbers to meet the men who had protected their families, and a lot of them even brought huge stacks of what was known as 'foot bread'. A giant naan-type sharing bread that was the first bit of fresh food some of us had eaten in a long time. The next morning was relaxed, and after eating a bread-filled breakfast, we extracted to where the choppers would pick us up and take us back to Camp Bastion. On our arrival at Camp Bastion, the snipers found out that Dan had been medically evacuated and that he had been returned to the UK. There was nothing we could do to help him, and we were gutted by the news. The war, however, was still raging, and so our focus soon shifted to our next operation.

The time spent in Camp Bastion was often the hardest part to deal with while on tour. A sense of normality would sneak into our consciousness and, with it, thoughts of home. Christmas Day had been a tough one for us. As we hastily ate a Christmas dinner off paper plates while sitting on wooden benches outside the cookhouse, we all began to think of home and our loved ones. We were deploying out on an operation on Christmas Day, which meant a quick call home to family and friends. This is where the mental strength of the troops came into play. Just imagine the person who lay their head on the pillow next to yours at night, or the parents who are worried sick while glued to the news, or the baby you held in your arms. They were all a million miles away but also just at the end of a phone line. Rare was the opportunity to call home, but when we did make those calls, it would be a little morale boost that would encourage us. It would feed the fire within us that burned so passionately for our homeland, but it was also a double-edged sword. Emotions would be stirred, and hearts would be broken. But for the men, there was no choice but to fight as hard as we could and make sure we returned home to our loved ones at the end of it all.

Smaller strike ops on Taliban positions and their commanders went on through the weeks, pushing the Taliban lines back, while simultaneously, the Americans were doing the same on the other side of the battlefield. Smaller strike teams began to deploy on operations with other units that needed them, and this included the snipers, who had been tasked to join a small Special Forces strike team and had flown off to our old hunting grounds from a previous tour the year prior. Thoughts of home seemed to creep in more and more as time went on, and the snipers found we had access to a satellite phone more frequently than we were used to at our new temporary base, so we used it a lot. A strange sense of split reality was the new norm for us as we kept our secrets to ourselves over the phone with our loved ones. Pointing out stars in the sky while on the phone to feel some sort of connection with the person on the other end. After a few days, we returned to Camp Bastion, and we were reunited with our battalion, who had now begun preparing for the next big operation. That operation would later be known as 'Operation Moshtarak', with a concurrent US operation taking place, later named the 'Battle of Marja'. The operation would be the biggest air assault to occur since WW2 and would consist of wave after wave of helicopters, dropping 15,000 troops directly on the Taliban's heads at their strongholds in Helmand Province, otherwise known as 'the green zone'. However, before they would deploy on Operation Moshtarak, there was one more job that needed to be done.

THE LONGEST DAY

An American Delta Force unit had been out to a suspected Taliban stronghold in a town that was unfamiliar to the Welshmen. The US troops had flown into the area to conduct a strike operation on a target. The American troops were instantly met by overwhelming enemy fire, which resulted in several serious casualties and deaths, including one of the chopper pilots. It was thought that the Taliban were in much stronger numbers than what had been originally reported, and this presented many problems. ISAF forces needed to know just how strong of an enemy force had congregated in the area, and there was only one way for them to find that out. The Welshmen would have to go in to kick the hornet's nest.

The sniper lads were divided up throughout the troops that were leaving for the impromptu operation, and each of the sections was briefed on what intelligence was known about the area and its fighters. The brief we received felt different to the ones previously given on the tour. The people giving these briefs weren't just some random military figure. They were men who were known to the troops, some for many years, and we knew the characteristics of that person and could tell something was up. This brief felt like it was riddled with danger and the almost daunting expectation of inevitable casualties and deaths. As the brief came to an end, the mentality of the snipers had shifted. This was a very serious situation that we were heading into. Not that previous situations had not been serious, but this time, it felt like we were being dropped into a gladiator arena, where certain death was lurking in the air, and the only way to avoid it was to fight harder than our opponents. That night, the men prepared their kit and made sure every single detail was as it should be. They had all been herded into one big tent to house all of the troops on the operation the night before deploying. All except for the snipers, who had some free reign and were undoubtedly trusted. Cigarettes smoked daily: 20.

Three-thirty in the morning, and we were awoken by one of the troops in the rifle company that had been sent over to the snipers' accommodation to grab us. We quietly collected our kit together and our weapons, then made our way out of the tents we shared with other fire support troops, being careful not to wake the other sleeping men around us who weren't going out on the operation that morning. That in itself was a strange moment, thinking how these lads could wake up and their friends could be dead. But I soon shook it off and we made our way over to meet the rest of the troops. We held our heads high as we walked over to the gaggle of men who were just about throwing on their kit and starting to head over to the airstrip where the Chinook helicopters would be waiting for us. Final checks were conducted, and the troops all began to load into the back of the helicopters. Tensions were high as we sat inside the noisy helicopters, mostly with our heads down. Some began to pray, and others, well, they took themselves to a very dark place. I sat with my head back against my seat, and I closed my eyes. My mind was going through every possible scenario that I could imagine facing me at the end of this flight. Today felt different, and today, unbeknown to me, would be the start of my revenge campaign against the Taliban for killing our friend Stevo just months earlier. The loss of Stevo was still fresh in us sniper boys' minds, and we were very aware that we might be about to meet the same fate as our dear friend. The flight would take just 30 minutes until we would reach the target drop zone, and as the minutes went by, the men became more and more laser-focused.

The early morning sky was still black as the two Chinook helicopters shot through the clouds, heading directly for the Taliban-held town. As they approached, the aircrew passed down the line, 'One minute!' The message was passed on to every man through the dim red lighting. The troops lifted their heads and took some deep breaths. I wasn't a religious man, nor did I know any prayers. I began to repeat something though that I'd heard somewhere, over and over in my head. 'As I walk through the valley of the shadow of death, I will fear no evil. For I will be the most evil bastard there!' And a quote from Genghis Khan. 'I am the punishment of the Lord. If you had not committed great sins, then God would not have sent a punishment like me upon you.' Suddenly, the Chinook pulled violently up and hard to the left. Then turned fully onto its side as a rocket-propelled grenade flew past. We had been spotted on our approach, and seconds after the RPG came bursts of heavy machine-gun fire that sent tracer rounds lighting up the cloudy sky like a scene from *Star Wars*. The Taliban were somehow ready and waiting for us, and they had seen the choppers coming way before the we would have liked them to have. This was a very well-protected and heavily armed stronghold. The two Chinook helicopters meandered through the air as bullets pinged off the sides of the metal plating. The side door and rear door machine gunners of both Chinooks had opened fire, sending thousands of rounds hurtling towards the multiple enemy positions. Right now, though, there was nothing that we could do, we just had to sit, wait, and hope we wouldn't be blown out of the sky.

A few moments passed, and the helicopters began to descend in an attempt to land us, if one of those choppers were hit, then it would have been devastating. Every machine gunner gave it their all, right up until the choppers both touched down in a muddy field right near the enemy positions. 'Go, go, go!' Shouted the aircrew as they signalled for us to run off the tailgate and onto the muddy field. The enemy rounds struck the outside of the helicopters as they tried to shoot inside the aircraft where we were all waiting. It was still pitch black outside as we ran off the choppers and took cover in the small recesses of the ploughed muddy field. Chaos erupted as troops lost their sections and their commanders in the darkness. Men froze in fear, and some found themselves wandering around in shock, clueless to the rounds flying past their heads. I had moved to the centre of the team I'd been attached to as the other snipers went off and joined theirs. In my kit, I had an infrared glow stick attached to a piece of string. The light was not visible to the naked eye, only to those using night vision. I knew the Taliban had night vision capabilities in some cases, but I needed to signal to the fast-approaching Apache attack helicopters that we were friendly and not an enemy position. The Chinooks pulled up and away as I began to swing the glow stick around my head. Suddenly, out of nowhere, everything fell quiet. The enemy fire had stopped, and the Apache helicopters soon left the area, having not fired a single round. It seemed like the Taliban had left and gone to reorganise and plan an attack or withdraw from the area completely. This gave the perfect opportunity for us to move into position and out of the hot drop zone.

We quickly left the open field and made our way down the side streets and alleyways towards the pre-designated compounds which we would commandeer. We would split into three groups, and each would take control of one of the compounds, creating a large triangular defensive position right in the centre of the district. I followed as my multiple left for our compound, searching every doorway and window as we moved and being careful to avoid improvised explosive devices. At the front of the patrol, the troops had already taken the compound where we would be staying and began to search it in depth, looking for any sign of the Taliban or any explosives. Smoothly and quickly, the Welshmen made their way into each of the rooms, and finally, they cleared the entire compound. It was safe, but now we needed to fortify the buildings so that they were ready to fight from. We pulled piles of sandbags from our kit and began to fill them with sand, placing them neatly on the roofs around the compound to create fire positions. We bashed holes through the walls so that more men could open fire at the enemy when the time came. I had chosen my location. A small side roof of a larger outhouse building would make for a good vantage point. From there, I was able to see up to the north and right around to the south-west. On the right-hand side of the building, lay the top of a treeline that followed a direct straight line up to the north as far as the eye could see. The other side of this treeline was being covered by another platoon and the other snipers who had taken over a compound further to the east. Directly in front of me, and next to the treeline, was an open ploughed field that stretched on for around 1,500 metres and ran parallel to a group of buildings over to the west. Directly to my west, I could see a long line of compound buildings that seemed to be the edge of a village. Nothing but 800 metres of open farmland separated my position from the buildings. Along the row of buildings ran a deep irrigation ditch, a dirt road which ran parallel, and a single tree. Two of the buildings stuck out slightly from the line and created a large quadrant-looking area which held a lone tree in the centre. As the hustle and bustle of troops preparing for battle went on below me, I took up my position on the rooftop and observed the area around me in preparation. I couldn't see behind me any further than the treeline extruding back into the streets and alleyways we had used to get to the compound that morning. It was a scary feeling not being able to see behind my position, but I had to stay alert as to what was happening in front of me and have complete trust that the men around me would keep me safe. Two of the lads, Pete and Vic, began to place sandbags around my position as I lay still and scanned the buildings over to the west through my scope. The sun was starting to rise over the trees just as something caught my eye.

The sun had reflected off a motorcycle in the distance over to the west. It was slowly making its way down the dirt road in front of the compounds from north to south. The only section of the road I could see was the area near the lone tree. As the motorcycle idled slowly down the road, the driver did not attempt to hide the fact that he was looking directly over at the compound housing us. 'I think we've got a dicker here, boss!' I shouted down to Captain Evans, the officer in command of the team. 'Keep an eye on him and report back, mate,' Evans replied. As I watched the area, I scanned up and down the road and started to gain a better understanding of the village in front of me. Another small section of road was visible to me in the far distance between two buildings, and something else had caught my eye through the scope of my weapon also. A minibus, with only a driver inside, was travelling north, but it gradually went out of sight. It was not uncommon for locals to throw what they could into their vehicles and get the fuck out of dodge before things kicked off, but this was just one man and no family. Suddenly, the motorcycle appeared again on the road near the lone tree. This time, there were two men on the bike, and they were heading south until they eventually went out of sight again. Moments later, the motorcycle returned with only the driver. 'Sneaky bastards,' I thought to myself. In the distance, I could see the minibus returning from up north, and this time it was full of fighting-age males. I then knew what was happening.

The Taliban were moving into position, ready to attack, and the motorcycle and minibus were dropping the fighters off at their positions and picking up the next wave. I was calling down from the roof to the boss on the ground, who was relaying the messages down the radio to HQ. 'I can see him dropping the cunts off on the bike. I'm going to let off a warning shot so he knows I can see him,' I said. 'Yeah, go on, Ted,' Captain Evans replied as he announced the shot down the radio. I had already dialled in some approximate turret settings on my scope for the distance to the road, and I began to breathe. Slowly, I entered my bubble, which had become such second nature by now. It was just like being back in Brecon on a stalk. I pulled back the bolt action of my weapon and chambered the .338cal sniper round. Safety catch off, and I slowed my breathing and heart rate right down. I followed the path of the motorcycle as it again came down the road from north to south. Leading the crosshairs of my sight just ahead of the bike by a metre or two as it moved steadily along. I let out half a breath, held it, and then squeezed the trigger. The round landed directly in front of the motorbike tyre, sending the rider into an almost uncontrollable wobble as he continued off down the road.

A few seconds later, and it had all started to kick off. A crescendo of noise erupted from all around us as cracks, zips, and whistles flew past my head and the other lads who were up on the rooftops across from me. Bullets smashed into the walls and the ground all around us and we were surrounded. The Taliban were everywhere, and they were certainly prepared for the fight. The American Special Forces operation must have given them a clue that this was going to happen, and the Taliban fighters gave us everything they had. Machine-gun fire and RPGs flew towards all three of the compounds occupied by the lads. The Welshmen had all been surrounded by Taliban units that had gathered in their hundreds. The troops returned a wall of rounds that rained down on the first wave of fighters, holding them back for the most part. Smaller fractions of the Taliban fighters, however, had broken off and attempted a skirmish attack through the alleyways with some success. The enemy had made their way to the maze of streets just behind me, but I couldn't turn around.

The ground troops fought like lions as the Taliban attempted to get close enough to throw their grenades over the walls. I had remained in my bubble of calm on top of the small outbuilding and methodically scanned the areas in front of me for shooters. There was nothing else I could do except to have total faith in my brothers behind me, and that's exactly what I did. I looked through my scope at the area surrounding the lone tree just as a single enemy fighter made a dash into cover in a section of low ground behind the tree. I watched as the insurgent raised his AK-47 from his hiding place and let off a burst of shots towards me and the other sharpshooters and machine gunners on the roofs of the compound. I took up my position, ready to return fire, as bursts of rounds were returned to the insurgent like a tennis match volley. I steadied myself, relaxed, and released my safety catch. My heart beating nice and slowly, and my breathing steady, I began to watch my crosshairs roll up and down the body and head of my target. Anger grew inside of me, but not like ever before. Everything about this single interaction, for some reason, felt personal, and almost like this one individual was the man responsible for the death of Stevo. A connection was made within my brain, and it was loaded with emotion.

Half a breath out, and bang! The round flew soaring through the air, but it missed. For just a moment, I had no idea why I had missed, and then it dawned on me. A small white plastic bag was tied to a stick at the edge of the field near the lone tree, and it was blowing in the wind. Instantly, I realised that the wind direction had changed since I had made my first adjustments to my scope. 'A few more clicks to the right should do it,' I said to myself. 'OK, here we go. Nice deep breath . . .' Bang! I'd sent the round spiralling through the air, kicking dusk up into my eyes from the muzzle. Through my dusty eyelashes, I watched intensely for the round to land. My head was cooking inside my helmet from the now several hours of hot sun that had been beating down on me since we arrived. Time seemed to slow down as the round landed. It had landed in the throat of the Taliban fighter, who had now dropped his weapon to the ground and was holding his neck with his hands. Blood squirted through his fingers as he reached out his left hand in the direction of the building nearest to him. I quickly turned my attention to the edge of the building, and sure enough, I saw something. There was another fighter hiding around the corner, and it looked like he was about to make a run for his fallen comrade. The first shooter collapsed into a heap on the ground, and the second insurgent made his dash from behind the wall towards him. I pulled back the bolt action on my rifle and aimed. This time, taking just a quick breath in and a short release, I let the round fly. I hit the second fighter straight in the chest, and the power of the vehicle-stopping .338cal round folded him in half backwards as his legs continued to run forward for a second. The anger I felt seemed to be alleviating any remorse or human emotion I might have felt towards the two dead men, and it changed something there and then. I could feel myself changing. Like some kind of bloodthirsty demon had just awoken, and it didn't plan on going anywhere for a very long time.

And so the day continued, and I continued to take the lives of the enemy fighters around me, as did the other snipers and rifle company troops that day, who endured relentless fighting at close range from the huge amount of enemy fighters in the area. As the sun began to dip in the sky, the fighting slowed down and eventually came to a complete stop. Why, we were not sure. But it was thought most likely that the Taliban had suffered massive casualties and could no longer stay in the fight. The troops could allow their bodies to slow down and take on some much-needed food and water after an excruciating 13-hour firefight for our lives. Before long, we had our kit on our backs and made the patrol back to the muddy field where the day had all started. The Chinooks swiftly returned, and wasting no time, the troops ran aboard for a quick take-off, carrying the injured on stretchers and helping the walking wounded. The journey back to Camp Bastion was one of solitude for most, unless helping to treat casualties on board. The sound of the Rolls-Royce engines drowned out any attempts to talk with one another.

The choppers landed on the Bastion airstrip, and we disembarked down the tailgate and onto the hot tarmac. As I walked exhaustedly off the back of the Chinook, I was met by a Land Rover waiting for me. Driving the vehicle was a British officer who introduced herself as the 'Media Liaison Officer . . .' and that I was to go with her. Clueless as to what was happening and still on autopilot from the effects of my lovely day out, I jumped into the Land Rover, and we drove off. We drove to a quieter area of the camp, and soon, we had come to a stop outside some site office cabins. 'OK, Ted, a few things before we go ahead here. You are about to be introduced to and interviewed by a member of the British press. You are not to answer any questions about casualties or air assets. OK.' 'Urm, yes, ma'am,' I replied. 'What exactly am I being interviewed about?' I asked the media liaison officer. 'Today,' she replied.

Barely able to keep my eyes open, I sat down at a small table, with a journalist from the UK papers sitting opposite me. The conversation was short and to the point. Talking about being a sniper and the effect I had on the ground in the fight against the Taliban. I proceeded to do as I was told and spoke openly about my day, but also something else which seemed to be skipped over. The mental effects that it was having on me and my dreams. I spoke of nightmares and the punishment I wanted to inflict on the Taliban. The interview was over in minutes, and I was taken back to my tent and the other lads from the support company who had not been on the operation that day. The newspaper report would knowingly be seen by the Taliban, who kept tabs on the British news to hear of any casualties. The write-up would be one of a warning to the enemy that this deadly sniper would be deployed on the upcoming gigantic operation and that now might be a good time to put down their weapons.

As I walked through the green canvas flaps of the accommodation tent, the room subtly cheered. Stories about me and the other snipers had already begun to circulate in the tents about our performance during the operation. We were welcomed back with open arms, and some even spent the time to check in on my headspace, which was hugely appreciated. As quickly as we could, we showered and changed into some clean clothes. The men who had not attended the operation waited for us before they left for the cookhouse. As we walked into the huge air-conditioned mess tent, shouts and cheers were heard throughout the rows of soldiers already eating who had heard about the day. The Welsh snipers had established ourselves as a force not to be messed with.

Many calls were made home that night as the troops tried to process the events of the day. There, however, was no time to sit around thinking about it too much. After all, we had to pack our kit and be ready to leave on Operation Moshtarak soon enough.

OPERATION MOSHTARAK

At four o'clock in the morning, waves of various nations' helicopters would shuttle-run thousands of ISAF troops into hostile territory. It was no secret to the Taliban that this attack was happening. The Welshmen would be the first to land at the target area, just outside of a village called Nad-Eali. The rest of the troops would follow during the rest of the day, except for some small Special Forces teams. It was the middle of the night when myself and the other snipers were awoken by one of the lads who'd been sent over from the rifle company to get us. This time, everyone in the accommodation tent was going on the operation. We threw on our gear and prepared our weapons. The day before had seen the biggest brief we had been a part of, and as the words 'Some of you may not return' echoed through our minds, we began to march. Thousands of troops marched towards the airfield, which had every kind of aircraft there at our disposal. Our accommodation tents were right next to the airstrip, so we didn't have far to walk, but the screeching sound of jets taking off all day and night was a pain in the arse, but it earned us an extra £5 a day in our paycheck at least.

I had been attached to my old rifle company, which meant I was back with some of my closest friends again. These were war-hardened men in the bodies of boys most of the time, as the American troops would describe us. Most were barely out of their teen years, but my God, could they fight. I had been assigned to the lead aircraft and the one to land first in enemy territory. On board were some of the best soldiers I knew, and with that confidence held by us all in one another's capabilities, we climbed aboard the Black Hawk chopper that awaited us.

The flight would take us over battlefields and burning buildings, heading deep into Taliban-occupied territory. As the first signs of blue skies broke from the darkness, so did the formation of helicopters that filled the sky. Eighty helicopters would make up the first wave of attack, but then suddenly, an alarm. The Black Hawk's radar had detected an incoming projectile, and it was heading straight towards our chopper. The alarm blared as myself and the other men held tightly to our weapons and seats. The side doors were open on the chopper, ready for a quick exit on landing. The Black Hawk shot off its chaff heat flares to evade the incoming missile. A sudden jolt, and the helicopter banked hard to the left. I lost my grip on the seat I was holding onto. There were not enough seats in the aircraft, so we had just squeezed onboard, and we had no seatbelts. The weight of the kit on my back pulled me towards the open door, which I was sitting right next to, my Bergan hanging out the side of the helicopter as Chris quickly reached out and gripped me by my straps and yanked me to safety. We all just laughed it off and carried on being thrown around by the evasive manoeuvres of the Black Hawk. A few minutes later, after shaking off the rocket attack, it was time to land, and we couldn't be happier to get off that bullet magnet.

The feet of the chopper just about touched down as I leapt out into some high grass, quickly followed by the rest of the blokes on the flight. Immediately, Chris and Tony started to plan the next move. The troops from all of the helicopters landed and took cover in the high grass and reeds that lined the main canal, which was heading parallel to the town. The landscape behind us was just open farmland on either side of the water, but on the opposite side to us were miles of compounds that went back as far as the eye could see.

Out of nowhere, the sound of a Tannoy speaker turning on was heard in the air, and a voice began to talk. 'What the fuck are they saying!' shouted one of the blokes. 'Get the interpreter to translate that for us,' said the boss. Mike, the Afghan-born volunteer interpreter, had come along with us to help as best as he could. He had good English and was hoping that his work with the British forces would lead to him being able to attend university in the UK after the war. He proceeded to tell us that it was the Taliban who were talking over the Tannoy. The speaker was situated on top of one of the many local mosques, and the Taliban were using it as a fortified position. Mike began to translate what the voice of the speaker was saying, and it was enough to send chills down your spine. 'They are telling the local people that they must leave now. They must leave now or join them in the fight. They must take their families and whatever they can carry and leave this place. They are saying there is going to be the holiest of wars here, and nobody's life will be spared if they stay and do not fight alongside the Taliban to defeat the infidels.' The interpreter looked worried as he passed on what was being said through the speaker. The voice continued to speak as movement in the town started to catch our eye. Donkeys, cars, motorcycles and anything that could move were being loaded with children and belongings. Animals tied together with camels leading from the front followed women holding ropes attached to them all, tugging while trying to care for their crying children. The local people were leaving, but not all of them. The Taliban would offer cash for new fighters, and this had tempted some to stay. Their commander continued to talk over the mosque's speakers, and he offered salvation to the British soldiers rather than a certain death.

This message had little to no impact on the war-hardened Welsh troops as we scanned the area for fighters, ready to pounce at a moment's notice. While the troops provided all-round security, the commanders made their plan. Just a few hundred metres to the south on our side of the canal was a large compound. It had several buildings, with a courtyard in the centre. The walls were high, and the location made for a perfect place to defend. The interpreter told us about how the Taliban intended a temporary cease-fire just while the villagers evacuated, and with that, the decision was made to move quickly. We headed for the compound, which we had chosen and, on arrival, were met by the owner, a middle-aged man who farmed the fields out to the west.

His family had already left their home some weeks earlier, and he planned to go and meet them. After a short conversation and some financial compensation, the man collected his things and took off on his little blue tractor across the fields. Not using the roads, he made a direct line into the horizon towards his wife. Immediately, we set about the various tasks needed to fortify the compound buildings and walls. Giant sandbag positions were built onto rooftops, and ladders were propped up against walls to provide extra fire positions in the event of an attack. It didn't take long for the new forward operating base to be up and running when we were joined by a platoon of French Foreign Legion troops. They would be operating in the area and would need to use the compound as their base for a little while. As the morning sun rose, all seemed to be quiet, and the troops got some hot food and a brew on. I had climbed on top of one of the roofs and had been watching over the area for enemy movements while the defensive positions were being built. The Foreign Legion blokes were preparing their kit to head out on their first patrol down below as myself and Sid lay in position watching the fields and buildings a few hundred metres to the south.

Out of nowhere, an RPG was fired from behind a wall, and it exploded above our heads, causing some minor shrapnel injuries to the men below. I tucked myself away behind my sniper rifle and pointed it in the direction of the shot. Together with Sid, I spotted a

Taliban fighter ducking down behind a wall and dumping the RPG on the ground next to him. I quickly evaluated the distance and wind between me and the target and dialled in the appropriate clicks on my scope. The insurgent popped back up from behind the wall, this time firing bursts of rounds from an AK-47 over the heads of Sid and myself. I quickly cocked the bolt of my weapon and chambered a round. 'What the fuck was that?' Andy reached the top of the ladder and dashed over to lay next to me. 'What's going on, mate?' he asked.

I briefed him on what had happened, and I was told to continue watching the target. As I looked back down my scope, I could see the target starting to run. The waist-high wall from which he had fired led across to a nearby building. The Taliban fighter had crouched down and made his way to that building. Once behind the building, he was no longer in my sights, and only a short 10-metre dash further across to the next building would provide enough cover for the target to disappear and never be seen again. I had a decision to make: fire when the opportunity arose or let the shooter get away for good after just attempting to kill me. A quick plan was made for a nearby air asset to track the insurgents. However, it was nowhere to be seen. 'Where's this air?' I shouted as the target appeared from behind the first building and started to run. I heard no reply as radio chatter was going on below me on the ground, and then suddenly, the target stopped, turned to face us on the roof, and waved at us. I blew out a deep breath of anger as I released my safety catch. I held the crosshairs on the target's chest and squeezed the trigger. The shot left no trace of the Taliban fighter except for the blood splatter against the high wall behind where he stood. The air assets never arrived, and I felt the demon inside my brain grinning as the adrenaline rushed through my body after taking yet another man's life.

The French Foreign Legion blokes had left the compound by now and headed back up north on a patrol, I had climbed down the ladder and sat down with the rest of the guys for a smoke. Shots rang out from north of our position, exactly where the French soldiers had moved to. I scrambled across the gravel, clutching my weapon and throwing it over my shoulder, the cigarette still burning at the side of my mouth. I sprinted towards the ladder made of tree branches and began to climb up to the roof. I'd reached the roof, however, without taking my helmet or body armour in the mad rush. The body armour made it difficult to shoot anyway, and I much preferred to shoot wearing my cap rather than a helmet that weighed my head down and fried my head with its black leather lining. Being able to send a round flying with accuracy at a long distance outweighed the need for safety in my head.

I lay down behind a small bunch of sandbags and began to try and spot the Frenchmen or the Taliban up to the north. I quickly scanned the area and spotted one of the legion troops. The firing had stopped, and the small French fire team were bounding their way back towards the forward operating base that was now known as FOB Ddraig. Or FOB Dragon, translated from Welsh. The Frenchmen burst through the compound doors and quickly withdrew to their quarters unharmed.

For days, the Welsh troops filled sandbags and built up our positions, all while knowing we were to be fighting to the death in the foreseeable future. The civilians who wanted to leave had done so, and only small pockets of locals remained. Every movement was observed with scrutiny as we played detective and tried to figure out what was happening in this place and where the Taliban were hiding. One day, I lay in my rooftop position observing the south along with one of the lads, Tez. Eight hundred metres to the south of our compound sat a mosque nestled into the outer lanes of the village. I had spotted someone on the roof of the mosque, crouching down and looking over in our direction. I made the appropriate changes to my sniper scope turrets and continued to watch the mysterious figure as I nudged Tez with my foot. 'I think we've got a dicker watching us over there, mate. A bloke is watching us on the roof of that mosque.' I passed my sniper rifle over to Tez so he could take a good look for himself. Tez agreed that the man was suspicious, and he handed the rifle back to me, and I immediately took up a firing position and continued to observe the man, who may well have been a Taliban fighter. The suspicious man pulled out a radio, and usually, in these situations, the radio messages would soon lead to mortar or Chinese rocket attacks.

Another life or death decision that had to be made, but this time not by me. The call was made by commanders to just observe the man and not engage. Moments later, the man climbed down from the rooftop and moved back into the village through the labyrinth of alleyways.

By now, Operation Moshtarak was well and truly underway, and troops started to mobilise to different areas of the district and operate in smaller units. Battles raged on around the area as the Welshmen fought back the Taliban, significantly disrupting their sickening plans. Huge stockpiles of IEDs were found, and multiple Taliban fighters were arrested and sent off for interrogation. Firefights raged on for more than 50 days as troops battled for ground by day and by night. The Welshmen took enemy position after enemy position, and we occupied the compounds that we took, fortified them, and made them home as best as we could. Every one of our locations were surrounded by the relentless Taliban fighters.

I had joined Andy's team as they left FOB Ddraig and headed down the canal to set up in an abandoned compound that was next to a local bazaar. The once-bustling marketplace had now been deserted. The town had been under Taliban control for quite some time, and their rule had brought with it a wave of destruction. Police and locals were being tortured, schools were being blown up, suicide vests were being strapped to children, and the list goes on.

The compound and the bazaar ran parallel to the main canal, as did the main supply route used by the ISAF vehicles. IEDs were a huge threat in the area, and every step had to be cleared by the metal detectors at the front of every patrol. To the east of the compound ran open fields, with trees and ditches running through them. The fields stretched on for over a mile until eventually reaching the edge of the next village. Farmland and thick vegetation surrounded the team's new location. This made for some possible routes which the Taliban could take to get close to the compound walls, and so we had to stay vigilant. Inside the large compound would be myself and Andy's team, the battalion mortar platoon, an Afghan Army platoon, and an Afghan Police section. Each of the units had our own quarters and objectives.

Me and the rifle company lads had our own section inside the large walls. Six small rooms in a row faced the eastern outer wall of the compound, which was also used as a rear entrance. A huge gap in the wall was barricaded with barbed wire, and a sentry position was posted next to it that would be manned 24 hours a day by the Welsh soldiers only. We built toilets and a shower area and tried to make life just that little bit better for ourselves. The toilets were made out of wooden chipboards, with a plastic toilet seat attached to them. We would then place our John bags inside, hanging from the seat. The poop bags would then be burned in a giant pit that burned 24 hours a day. The tricky part was trying not to piss in the bags, well, that was if you wanted to prevent having piss steam floating around the place. The shower area consisted of a brief privacy screen and a wooden pallet on the floor. The shower itself would come from solar bags, a five-litre translucent bag with either a black or a silver lining. The bags, which, when left in the scorching sun, would heat the water to a decent enough temperature. Showers, however, as well as clothes washes, were a rarity. The water would need to be made up of leftover bottled water, of which we would be rationed two bottles daily. It could take weeks to save enough water to shower, and when the chance came, we would shower initially in our dirty clothes to make the most of the water. Food and water could not be refrigerated or kept cool anyway, and so after a while of living in such harsh conditions, the we began to experiment. We found that wetting a sock and using it to hang a water bottle in the sun would partially cool the water inside as it evaporated. This amazed us young Welshmen, who were just about to have our minds blown by our Fijian brothers hand-fishing crabs from the small waterways. Melons grew in some of the vegetated areas, but they were rare to find. Weeks had gone by of fighting and patrolling the area and with some positive effects.

As the troops established our hold on the area, we also made sure to speak to the locals and get to know them and their stories. Having meetings with village elders and meeting the local children would bond them and us. Over time, we developed a relationship with the families, and we provided as many books and school accessories to the children as we could carry. This infuriated the Taliban, who had been targeting schools throughout the area, but the children had a burning desire to have an education. After some time, the local bazaar had started to reopen some of its stalls, and this meant the rare chance for us to buy some fresh food.

We had been living for weeks on food that was squeezed from a foil bag, so fresh meat and vegetables could be a huge, much-needed boost to morale. Our rations just needed to be boiled in a bag, and so the need for cooking equipment was moot. So the question arose: how would we cook any fresh food we may get our hands on?

We began to collect wire and empty ammunition tins and set to work our imaginations. Having creative tasks to do was a great way to divert the mind to somewhere other than the war. We made deep fat fryers by making chip cages out of wire and the larger ammunition tins to hold oil. We gathered up dirt and sand, mixed in some water, and built it up all around another ammunition tin that had a space underneath for a fire and a little chimney to create an oven. As soon as the soil hardened in the scorching sun, it was time to go shopping.

A small group of lads made their way carefully over to the marketplace to buy oil, potatoes and a chicken. The locals were so happy to see them integrating into their day-to-day lives, and the local guys freshly butchered a chicken and gathered some oil and potatoes. That night, we sat around the fire and had a small feast. However, the sudden addition of rich foods into our diet caused stomach issues for most throughout the night.

Firefights and patrols were the norm through the months, and the weather continued to get hotter. Temperatures above 50 degrees Celsius were recorded as we carried around our 80lb packs on our backs for miles. This gained us the nickname 'Donkeys' from the

Taliban, along with a few others. The average night's sleep was four to six hours, usually broken up because of stag duties, patrols or attacks. Phone calls home became weeks apart, and the war was starting to take its toll on all of the men. We had all lost significant body weight due to the mass amount of calories we used daily, in addition to the blistering heat. Our rooms were infested with camel spiders, scorpions and snakes. Night-time operations had become more frequent, as we hunted down the Taliban fighters and overwatched the villagers as they slept. Later, we would be referred to as the ghosts in the night, that you cannot see, but you know are there.

One night I had been on sentry duty in the middle of the night, I had been hearing fire fights rage on in the far distance and seen the occasional tracer round flying through the sky. I made my way quietly back in to my room and sat on my bed to take off my boots. I lay my weapon on the floor next to my body armour and helmet, and placed them all neatly in the same position as always. Everything was always ready to go at a second's notice, and that went for all of the lads.

I climbed into my sleeping bag and lay there for a moment and thought about everything that had happened on the tour so far, and how life was back at home. I eventually drifted off to sleep, exhausted from being awake all night.

Boom! Boom! Boom! Suddenly, I was awakened by the room trembling and dust falling from the ceiling. Boom! Another huge blast went off, and I raced to grab my weapon. It was still dark as I shouted to wake the other lads in the room, who were in a deep sleep and still groggy. 'We're getting bumped lads!' I shouted, and with that I pulled the bayonet from my body armour and made my way to the door. Boom! Another explosion shook the room.

'Get the fuck up!' I shouted, and with my foot I opened the door. I had my sniper rifle, but that was no good up close in the dark, and so I held my rifle with my left hand, and my bayonet in my right. I was ready to fight, and the lads from my room were not far behind. I stepped out into the darkness and scanned the courtyard for enemy fighters. I couldn't see anything or anyone, and so I ran into the next room down to make sure everyone was getting up.

I looked across and saw Andy through an open doorway on the radio. I made my way in to the room. 'Andy, what do you need me to do?' I asked, but something didn't seem right. Tom was sat next to Andy and turned to face me and laughed. 'It's the fucking mortars lads firing mate.' I couldn't believe it, and I felt slightly embarrassed, but now at least I knew what I would do if it ever happened in the future.

THE ONE-MILE SHOTS

One afternoon, as we recovered from a long foot patrol in the sun, a burst of shots was heard in the far distance. A pretty common occurrence, but, after overhearing a short firefight, a message was relayed over the radio. The unit under fire began to brief Andy on what had just happened just as he grabbed me. 'Can you jump up on the roof, mate, and have a look out over that direction? I'm being told the enemy could have moved towards those far buildings to the east.' 'Yeah, of course,' I replied, and I grabbed my weapon and ran up the ladder that was propped up near the front gate defensive position. I darted across the rooftop, which was always a daunting task, for fear of being shot in plain sight by an overlooking enemy sniper. I dived onto the roof where used syringes of heroin lay, discarded by the Taliban who had been there in the past.

I took up my position and started to scan back and forth over the huge fields and among the buildings at the edge of the village, far to the east. Moments later, I was joined by one of the lads, Sid. He provided a relay to the troops on the ground, who were looking up at me. Suddenly, I spotted something move, which caught my eye, although I couldn't tell what it was at first. I began to create my bubble, but to do so, I needed to focus and also feel safe to be in such a vulnerable place. Sid provided that feeling of safety that I needed and observed the landscape surrounding me for any approaching enemy.

Just days before, while our compound was under attack, me and Sid had risked it all together for the greater good. Enemy fire had been raining down on our compound, and the threat of grenades being thrown over the wall was ever-increasing. Nobody could see where the shots were coming from, and so I again made a choice. In just my shorts and flip-flops, I quickly swapped weapons with one of the riflemen. Now armed with an SA80 rifle, I ran towards the compound gates. Immediately, I was followed by Sid, who was in the same attire. We both dashed out of the compound gates and headed out around the corner, we planned to draw the enemy fire, allowing the rest of the troops to see the enemy position and neutralise it.

I lay on the roof behind my rifle and began to observe the wind as it moved over the fields in front of me. It seemed to be blowing in three different directions, between me and the buildings in the distance. This meant that to prepare my scope for accurate firing, I would have to make three separate wind calculations and average them. As well as these equations, I would also have to take into account the temperature, altitude, biometric pressure, and distance while making adjustments to my scope. The distance to the first row of buildings was over a mile. So, if a shot was going to be made, then it was going to be a difficult one.

I took my time making my adjustments and then continued to scrutinise every dark hiding spot or bit of cover in the far distance. The sun, by now, had started to set, casting an orange glow over the land. 'Mate, I've got someone. There's three of them, with weapons,' I said to Sid, who in turn passed the message down to the ground, and Andy, who was on the radio. 'Air assets are a while away, Ted, apparently, so keep your eyes on those fuckers!' he shouted. I began to take deep, long breaths and pulled my cap down over my eyes to shield myself from the low-setting sun. The three enemy fighters had moved out of view, and with every minute, the sun was dropping lower, and darkness began to set in. 'I need some light over there, mate,' I said. The mortar platoon was unable to fire due to the imminent arrival of air assets in the area. The lads, however, did have bright white flares that they could fire over towards the targets' location. They would fall slowly to the ground using small parachutes and would light up the area for just a few minutes. The night flares soared audibly through the air, and they illuminated the ground below. However, they couldn't reach quite as far as I needed them to, Leaving me just a dim glow to work with. Then suddenly, in walked the three insurgents, heading from north to south past the row of buildings inside the picture of my scope.

I could see their AK-47s down by their sides as they walked calmly in single file down the dirt track. I thought the single-file formation would more likely be due to IEDs that had been placed in the area to catch the British troops who may follow them after having been attacked. As I watched the men, both the front and rear, they seemed to be controlled by the man in the centre.

Up ahead in the direction the Taliban were heading was a small alleyway that led deep into the village and then out of sight. There was only a small window of opportunity to make these shots, and with that,

I released my safety catch and I entered my bubble. The distance to the target would mean I had to maximise the elevation turret on my scope. Maximum clicks meant I had to aim off the target, and the intended insurgent would not be visible to me as I squeezed the trigger. I began to slow my breathing and felt as my heartbeat slowed too. Every muscle in my body had to be perfectly aligned, and my mind was in an almost deep, meditative state. Everyone was deathly quiet around me. A heavy, long breath released from my sunburn-puckered lips, and I squeezed the trigger, sending the round flying off into the evening sky. I regained my composure just as the all too familiar ringing in my ears started to fade, and the dust cleared from my eyes. I saw the round splash in the dirt, just inches behind the third insurgent. A few more clicks to the right, and I knew the next round would hit its target.

I had already made a plan of how this was going to go down. I would shoot the target at the rear of the group first, hoping to pick him off without too much disturbance to the other two targets. Then quickly, half a breath out, and bang! The round struck the man in the chest and violently threw him to the floor. I reloaded my rifle rapidly. The rear target lay on the floor, dying, as the next two turned around to see him. A distance of 1,456 metres would mean there would be a time delay between the round hitting the target and them hearing the initial shot from the rifle.

I moved my crosshairs across to the man at the front of the group, who seemed to be frantically talking with what appeared to be his superior next to him. Bang! I fired another shot, and it again pierced through the target's chest, collapsing him to the now blood-soaked ground from the previous target's body. The central target began to run, well as best as he could anyway. I had never seen a 100-metre flip-flop race before, but this guy would have definitely made the Olympic team. I pulled back the bolt of my weapon and chambered my next round. I knew where this guy was running to, and it almost felt unfair. I moved my crosshairs over to the nearby alleyway entrance, where seconds later, the final target would appear. With a slow squeeze of my trigger finger, I had sealed the fate of yet another man, and as the shot burst through the torso of the petrified man, running for his life, a message was passed over the radio.

'You tell that sniper that was some damn good shooting,' an American accent said. An Apache helicopter had been in the area and witnessed the shots hit their targets at over a mile away. Andy passed on the message to me, as I was now making my way down off the rooftop. The troops on the ground were thrilled with what had just unfolded, and they congratulated me on my endeavour and the shots

I had just pulled off. I walked off without saying a word to anyone, around the corner, then sat in the courtyard area outside of my room. I sat alone and smoked cigarette after cigarette, with my eyes wide open, staring into nothingness. The guys all thought it best to leave me to decompress and go about their usual routines. I didn't move or stop smoking for hours. After a while, I could hear a faint conversation in the distance, and the interpreter, Mike, had a radio message to pass on, which he had intercepted from the Taliban. One of the three men I had killed had been a Taliban commander, and Mike had heard the dead commander's brother talking to their fighters over the radio, vowing to avenge his death. As harrowing as this could sound, I was unaffected by the news and welcomed the fight with my head held high, even leading a night patrol myself in the hunt for the challenge.

Days and nights went by of sporadic firefights in the area, but I remained quiet and distant. A rage was building within me, and my thoughts were distorted by so many contributing factors that it had exhausted me. I had started to wake up screaming in my sleep, and the happy-go-lucky, forever joyful lad that everyone knew was nowhere to be seen.

My eyes were dead, and the only thing I thought about was killing. I was a creative person, and from that passion, I began to draw. I began to draw my dreams and also began to vocalise them into poems which would only be seen by my eyes. Depicting scenes of horror and torment that had been living in my mind for some time now. Worsening with every battle or sleepless night, thinking about what I had done. Everybody noticed the change in me and my demeanour. I kept my mouth shut and continued to do my job, unknowing that just one more firefight would send me over the edge.

Tony and Andy had begun to discuss my situation over the radio after a prompt from Sid, and as both men knew me well, it was easy to see that something needed to be done. One of the mortar blokes, Jack, had been Trauma Risk Management – TRM – trained, which meant that he was the first point of call for a situation like this. Trauma Risk Management was intended to assess the symptoms of mental health injuries, and as Jack sat down to talk with me, he was beyond shocked at the results. Jack had never seen scores so high and immediately reported his findings to Andy and Tony, who both agreed that something needed to be done quickly.

I looked like a shaking bag of nerves and had developed some very serious mental health symptoms. The anger was driving me 24 hours a day, and it was feeding the demon who had now taken full control, and it was relentlessly hungry for more death.

Leaving my friends in the wake of my destruction, I was to be medically evacuated back to FOB Ddraig, where I would be reunited with old friends and, hopefully, a little lift to my morale.

I was picked up from my compound and taken down the canal road, feeling like I had let everybody down. How had this happened, and what was going to happen to me now? Mental health issues would quite often lead to the end of someone's career, and this weighed heavy on my mind.

Two brothers Dean and Rick that I knew from back home cooked me some food and tried their best to cheer me up back at the FOB, but the light inside of me was gone. I was a shell of myself, and the following morning, I saw a helicopter come to evacuate me and take me back to Camp Bastion. The flight back to camp was short, and I began to cry for the first time. I didn't know why I was so emotionally broken, and I was terrified of the repercussions of my medical evacuation. The chopper touched down, and I was whisked off to the medical centre at Bastion. Blood-stained floors and severely injured troops screaming in pain were to meet me on my arrival. A Medical Evacuation Black Hawk helicopter had just landed some troops who had sustained catastrophic injuries and the place was crazy.

Ten minutes after my arrival, I was called in to speak with a psychiatric nurse. We spoke about what I had been doing, my symptoms, my feelings, and my darkest thoughts. The conversation was short and abruptly ended in being told that I was more than likely just over-tired, with what sounded like a possible addiction to killing, and that I should be sent to work in the stores for a couple of weeks to catch up on my sleep. Medical chit paper in hand, I travelled on the camp bus service to my accommodation tent, where I would sit alone, sleep alone, and eat alone until a few days slowly passed by, and I was collected for my new job role in the stores.

TWO BIRDS, ONE STONE

The other snipers had been hard at work, spread out along the front lines they battled with the Taliban. Being the assets that we were to our units, the snipers all felt pressure on our shoulders.

We were usually the ones with the best optical capabilities and the ones with the ability to make the furthest shots, and so naturally we became the first port of call for every firefight. This often led to us putting our lives on the line in order to do what we were capable of doing.

One hot afternoon Gray had been tasked to accompany a team in clearing a section of buildings. As the team cleared one of the suspect compounds, rounds began to crack and zip over their heads. They had come into contact from the West, and without hesitation Gray climbed a ladder up to the top of the wall and began to search for the culprits.

The bullets whistled past his head as he scanned the area for the Taliban fighters, but in his zone of concentration, he had put himself directly in the centre of the enemy fire. Rounds landed all around him, kicking dust all over him. Gray stayed silent and composed, oblivious to his near-imminent death.

Suddenly, he was grabbed from behind by the ankles. The men below could see the rounds splashing all around him, and they pulled him down from the wall that was now riddled with bullet holes.

We all found ourselves in the most dangerous of situations, and the sound of bullets flying inches past our heads had just become a work related irritant by now. We all had our own little bubbles, and those bubbles allowed us to accomplish the battle-winning, war changing feats that we did.

While inside his bubble, Gray had lay atop a compound roof while taking heavy fire, some weeks after his near-death experience. He scanned a cluster of buildings as ground troops came under attack below him from various positions around 900 metres away from his location.

A dusty track ran parallel to open fields until it hit the group of buildings, and a team of troops had been held back from advancing up the road by the Taliban fire. The area had been a hotspot for activity and was indeed a Taliban stronghold.

The buildings were littered with enemy murder holes, a tactic that allowed the Taliban to shoot and not be seen and to also remain behind the thick walls in cover from British fire. Gray scanned the murder holes, struggling to peer inside the dark buildings. It was hard to pinpoint just where exactly the firing was coming from, and then he spotted it.

A doorway to the building was facing him, and he began to peer through the opening from the door being ajar. He could see that someone was moving inside. Gray began to calculate the corrections he would need to make to his scope and quickly dialled them in. He slowed his breathing, and watched through his scope as the door began to move.

Suddenly, a Taliban fighter made a move to dash out of the door, and Gray released his safety catch. Half a breath out, and he squeezed the trigger, sending the .338 round hurtling through the air. Just as the dust cleared, he saw something that he was not expecting. The round had pierced through the insurgent's chest yes, but just as it did so, another fighter came to view in the doorway.

The round smashed through the first fighter's chest and went straight through the second one. He had shot two Taliban with one bullet, and suddenly all fell quiet. It seemed as though the once-thought-impregnable Taliban stronghold was no match for the Welsh sniper, and the Taliban had retreated off through the rat tunnels and surrounding buildings.

Suddenly Gray spotted something heading down the road towards the ground troops just 20 metres away from where he was positioned. He frantically scanned the road and spotted what it was that he had seen. A man was pushing a wheelbarrow down the road, and instantly, Gray relayed what he had seen over the radio.

Something was hanging out of the wheelbarrow, and as Gray zoomed in through his scope, he could see it was a leg that was coming over the side of the wheelbarrow. A second wheelbarrow then followed shortly behind the first, and it had another body in it.

The first body was clearly dead however the second was still clinging on to life. As a British soldier, the men had the duty and obligation to give the enemy fighter medical assistance. He was initially treated on the ground while the troops waited for a medical evacuation helicopter to arrive and take the man back to Camp Bastion for further treatment.

Radio chatter had been ongoing throughout the event, and assets in the sky had watched the whole thing unfold. The compound had been under watch for some time prior, and Gray would be needed to return to Camp Bastion also to be questioned on what had just happened.

The helicopter arrived, and the Taliban casualty was loaded onto the back, followed by Gray. He sat down as the chopper took off, leaving just him and the dying combatant in the back. There was no crew in the back of the chopper, just him and this guy he had just shot.

'What the fuck,' Gray said out loud and he sat with his head back against his seat until they landed. Richie was back at Bastion and later informed Gray that the Taliban fighter had later died of his injuries.

Meanwhile, back at Camp Bastion, I was still struggling with my mental health but had at least now been given something to do. Dave was a guy from my previous rifle company who worked in the stores, and he was just the kind of guy I needed to be around after returning from the front lines. An upbeat, easy-going guy who didn't have much for me to do except help out a little bit with moving stuff around in the shipping container stores unit, but at least it was something. One perk to the mind-numbing store work was that the immense heat inside the metal shipping containers was so unbearable that an extra £5 a day would be added to our wages. A few more days passed, and the troops out on the ground were still hard at it. Pushing the Taliban back as they took more and more ground in the raging war that had now seen the Welshmen take more and more casualties.

Dave and me had been tasked to fly out to a small operating base near the town of Sangin and handle some equipment there that may be needed by the advancing British troops. I felt useless as I sat on my bed day after day in the well-equipped camp. Not being out on the ground was driving me crazy, and I started to feel the hurt that was inside of me. Then Dave received a call. 'I hope this means we are getting a job,' I thought to myself just before Dave walked back into the tent.

'Hey mate, sit down for a second,' Dave said as I perched myself eagerly on the edge of my bed, ready to hear what was next for us. 'I've got something I need to tell you, mate. Jonny has been hit, and it's bad.' The world felt like it had begun to cave in, and I just about managed to get out the words, 'How bad?' Through my gritted teeth. Dave looked at me and gently said, 'It's pretty bad, mate, I don't know too many details, apart from it being an IED, and there were a few casualties, but Jonny is the most critical, and he has been evacuated to the UK. I think he's lost limbs, mate.' I stood up, took a deep breath and quietly said, 'OK, mate, cheers'. I walked outside, devastated by the news of

Me, Slater and Dan on an observation lesson in Brecon, south Wales.

Con, me and Andy just about to leave Camp Bastion with the Mobile Reconnaissance Force.

Me sat on top cover behind the grenade machine gun of our Jackal vehicle as we head through the desert to a target.

Me overwatching an enemy position as we take cover from Taliban fire in an irrigation ditch.

Bennie, Jenks, myself and Gray catching a quick photo before heading out on a strike op. Gray with a cat's arse sausage roll hanging out of his mouth.

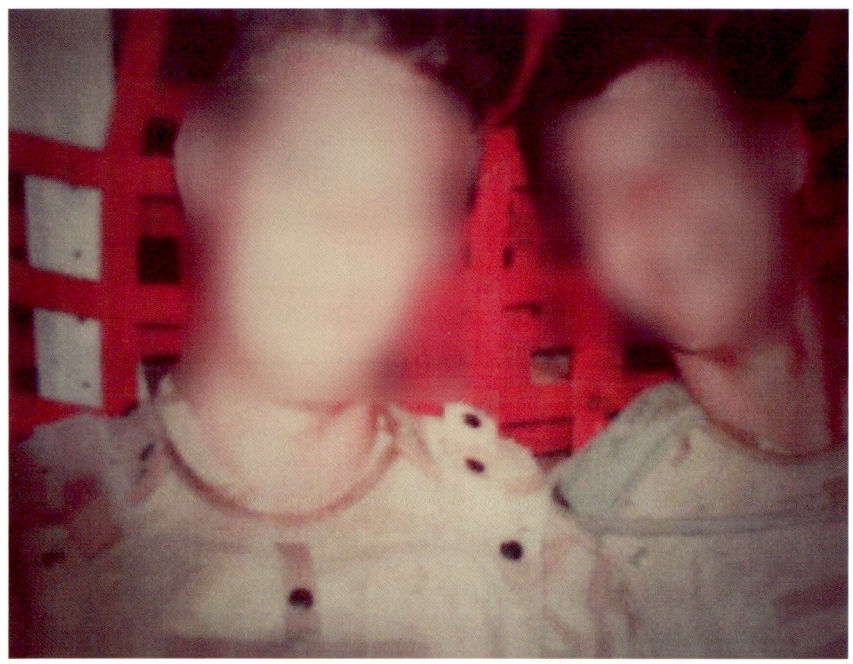
Me and Dan in the back of a Chinook after an op.

Adi, Jenks and Bennie providing cover for troops as they extract out of enemy fire.

Me observing a potential enemy position as Estonian troops advance to investigate.

Gray scanning for Taliban fighters as ground troops advance into battle.

Bennie observing enemy movements from the shadows.

Jenks in his rooftop sniper hide.

Me on the rooftop of FOB Ddraig as Operation Moshtarak kicks off.

Me lying on the rooftop just before an RPG and AK-47 rounds got fired overhead.

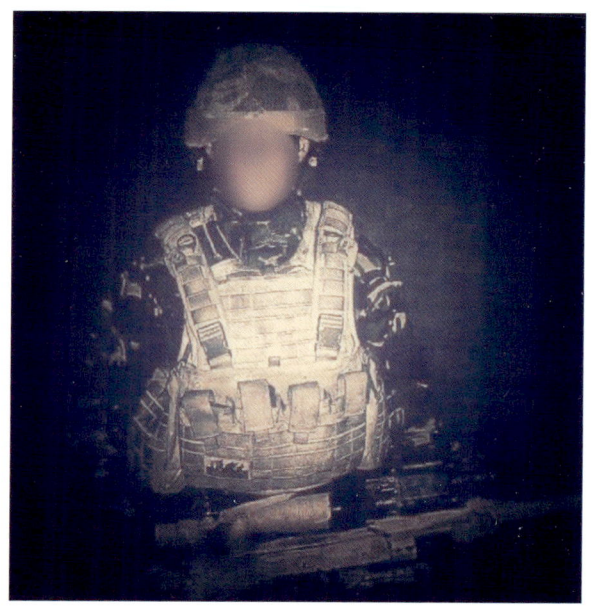

After a long night of patrolling, me and the lads make it back to our FOB.

Me and some of the lads playing cards while we wait for something to happen.

After returning from a night recce and the rare chance I didn't have my trusty sniper rifle.

A Chinook helicopter drops us off a much needed resupply of food, water and ammunition. Except all the meals were bloody corned beef hash. Disgusting.

The mortar lads making a noise. This one I knew about.

Gray taking a knee as a chopper is inbound.

Me and Jenks smoking our cigars on the beach in Cyprus.

Me and Harry ride a tuc tuc through the streets of Bangkok.

Me and one of the boys soaking in the culture at a temple in northern Thailand.

A small jungle village in northern Thailand where we met the 'long neck' people of the local tribe.

Me and the gang dropping of some school supplies at a remote village in the jungle. We spent the next day helping to pick coffee beans with the farmers on the hillside.

Our little cabin on the sheep farm in Australia.

Me and the boys on a scorching hot New Year's Day in Brisbane. This is the second floor living room of our house.

Smashing out the tunes on the yacht while taking in the sights of Portugal's southern coast.

Me and the gang at the summit of a mountain in the Rockies of Canada.

Marge taking it all in as we stop off in America.

Me after breaking through the smoke barrier of wildfires. We camped over at the Yosemite National Park just below.

my close friend's life-threatening condition and anxious to hear how he was doing or if he would even survive the blast.

Days passed in the quiet base where I had been sent to relax when the news came of another casualty. This time, though, the injured Welshmen died from his injuries. It dawned on me that Dan, who was at home recovering, had no idea what was happening to the lads out in theatre. I had to pick up the phone once the lines opened back up and pass on the news, just as Dan had done for me months earlier. The conversation was short, and both of us held back our emotions as we spoke about what details we could. Dan, me and Jonny had been close friends for years now, and the realities of young men going to war were slapping us in the face.

The frustration was unbearable for me, I just wanted to get back out and fight alongside my friends and do my best to protect them. Soon, though, it was time to return to Camp Bastion and be reunited with a few of the troops that had returned from Operation Moshtarak. Seeing the lads seemed to cheer me up slightly as we went about our days in camp, making the most of what food was on offer and the fast food that was screaming out to us malnourished troops.

A brief had been called by Tony, who had now returned from the front lines with many of my closest friends. The end of our tour in Afghanistan was closing in, and one word was on everyone's minds: complacency. Complacency was a killer, and right now was the time to be most aware of it as the tour approached its end. However, there was one more job that needed to be done before we headed home. An operation on the outskirts of the operational area, where the Taliban still had a fleeting resistance. With just days left in Afghanistan, Tony asked who would volunteer for the final operation. I immediately threw my hand straight into the air. 'I'm in!' I shouted as a bunch of other guys also threw up their hands. I couldn't stand the thought of not going back out to the front line, and so I convinced everyone that I was OK. A decision was made by the chain of command that I would be sent back to the medical centre, and I would have to get the OK from the psychiatric nurse before being allowed to deploy.

I sat calmly in front of the same nurse who had told me I was just tired and answered his questions as if nothing was ever wrong. I even agreed with him that all I needed was a good rest, but now I was ready to get back out there. My return to the fight, however, came with a condition that was imposed by the psychological assessment team and also agreed on by my commanding officers. I was to hand in my sniper rifle and deploy with only my assault rifle, the reason for which was never explained, but I had my thoughts on why that may have been.

The orders for the last operation were to provide security to a main supply route that had been the target of many enemy IEDs. We flew out by Chinook to the area and travelled along the long, dusty supply route by foot. Looking up at the high walls of compounds used by another unit from the battalion, we could see thousands of bullet holes and scorch marks. This place was certainly not to be underestimated, and the we had to stay switched on right until the end. Me and the guys all reached our checkpoint, introduced ourselves to the troops already there, and set up our room for the night.

Days went by with little to no Taliban activity, and this angered me beyond belief, as I wanted to inflict revenge on as many of the Taliban fighters as I could before my tour was over. Something huge had changed in me by now, like a dark side that had taken over me, and it had changed who I was at my very core. A side that thrived in violence and was addicted to it. Always operating at full steam and constantly scanning for targets like a heartless cyborg. No compassion or empathy existed in this monster that I'd become. The darkest of desires fuelled me as I would overwatch the surrounding fields and treelines in the hope of an attack or just the opportunity to take another life. Like an addict, I sat tense and undistracted from my one goal. Execution. The job, however, came to an end without a single round being fired by myself or the other men in the compound. The last piece of action I would see in Afghanistan would be the vaporisation of two Taliban fighters, hit with a missile from a Predator drone while digging to bury an IED in the road. The missile would turn the two men into a pink mist that just blew away in the wind. Days later, I would be stood naked on the table of my local pub, surrounded by my friends and family, while trying to act as normal as possible. Cigarettes smoked daily: 70.

The final operation was coming to an end, but not without one last drama for the lads. The weather had started to take a turn for the worse. Wind speeds were rapidly increasing, and the skies began to turn dark. Soon, we could smell something familiar in the air. Our kit was packed and ready to go, and we had a slight spring in our step as we awaited the Chinook helicopter to take us back to Camp Bastion. Suddenly, there it was. A giant wall of dust, towering hundreds of feet high, was engulfing everything in the far distance. A sandstorm was rolling in, and we knew first hand just how horrendous they could be. Just as the conversation between the lads turned to whether or not the chopper would come, a message came over the radio. The flight had been cancelled, and we would be staying out in the green zone for at least another night. The storm turned out to be a short one, luckily for us, and the very next day saw us leave the front line for the final time.

HOMEWARD BOUND

Before we could land in the UK, we needed to spend two days decompressing. 'Decompression' was a period spent at our old base on the island of Cyprus, where we would be issued with two beers each and entertained by a stand-up comic and some live music. We sat on the beach and smoked cigars as we planned how to spend all the cash we had saved up. The reality, though, was that a car, a holiday, some clothes, and enough alcohol to sink a ship were all that would be to show for our time spent in Afghanistan. Well, that, and the demon which had now attached itself to most of us. Carving images into the back of our skulls. The time in Cyprus was strange, like a forced kind of fun. Nobody held a deep or meaningful conversation; we just sat dazed for the most part. Some planned the next chapter of their life. Some ticked off yet another tour of duty. Some of those young men, well, they were about to start a very different kind of war.

The snipers had, without a doubt, made a huge impact during our time in Afghanistan, and many lives had been saved and firefights won because of us. The past six months had taken its toll on each of the lads, and the pressure and responsibility of our job, well, that was a tremendous burden to bear. Each of us had achieved absolute professionalism, and each had made noteworthy actions on the battlefield, as well as demonstrating some extraordinary shooting. We could hold our heads high, yet our heads felt heavy.

During a firefight, I would enter my 'bubble', and that would almost disassociate me from reality. The reality was that I was in incredible danger, and rounds were literally within inches of my head regularly. However, my reality saw me protected by my absolute belief that I would be fine, no matter the danger in front of me. Coexisting with that belief was the knowledge that myself and everyone around me had trained extremely hard for the situation, and we all had each other's back. That ability to disengage with reality yet perform to such a high standard was key to our success.

Something which became apparent to me later in reflection was how each time I entered the 'bubble' state, the longer the effect would last. It wasn't until landing back in the UK that I realised my cognitive state. All of a sudden, I was surrounded by the sight of green grass and the smells of home. In comparison to where I had just come from, it was otherworldly. Afghanistan, for the most part, was a barren desert land, and so the fresh smell of the British vegetation was like going from black and white to colour TV. It awoke senses and emotions that had been switched off, and with that, I snapped back to reality. I had been in a daze for weeks now, like my eyes had sunken into my head, and I could just watch from inside as something else took control. The reality check came as a pretty big blow, and after my world spinning for a while, it eventually settled in this half-and-half reality, like a heavy stage curtain had dropped on my head, splitting me into two very different worlds. One half was filled with love and adoration from the people now around me, and on the other side, I was still fighting for my life. All of this came crashing down onto me like a wave, but I didn't say a word. I knew the slightest wrong word could see my career over and the end of my further plans for Special Forces selection. A dream I had held since I was a child and a promise I had made to myself.

I fought with my consciousness and battled to remain in the real world and not the war zone reality inside my mind. Years later, I would find that many of the people around me were doing the very same thing. Holding onto a sliver of reality while living and working in a place where aggression is encouraged, alcohol is a pastime, and the best thing to focus on was the next deployment back to Afghanistan the very next year. All that while trying to replicate the person we used to be around loved ones and trying to fit seamlessly back into civilisation, as if awoken from hypnotisation where the feelings of love, compassion, and empathy had all been removed.

Weeks began to go by at home, and the darkness I felt seemed to be only getting stronger, and it had started to manifest itself in ominous ways. Mostly, it would manifest in an uncontrollable anger that would consume me within a millisecond and would often lead to violent outbursts and aggressive reactions to the slightest of things. After all, those are the things that had just kept me alive. I would wake up screaming from nightmares that would start up every single time I slept, which would often lead me to go days without sleep at all. Trying to keep my struggle hidden from my family and friends was starting to wear me down and became ever increasingly difficult.

Alcohol became a crutch, and I soon found myself with a bottle of whisky by my bedside each night. I would fly into fits of rage with the other troops around me for no apparent reason, and no matter what I did, I couldn't shake this feeling that something was dangerously close to taking over my mind completely.

Army life in the camp continued as though nothing had ever happened and that visiting friends with who now had no limbs in hospital beds was all just a part of the job. No 'How are you?' talks or mental welfare checks. The main concern held for the returning troops was our high statistic for being involved in road traffic collisions or drunk-driving incidents. Explained to us as a result of us feeling unstoppable after an operational tour and that we were now more likely to take risks. Another view could be that most of the returning troop's minds were still on that battlefield.

THE ARMOURY

One monotonous morning in camp, the troops from my company headed over to the armoury to collect our weapons for cleaning. I signed out my sniper rifle, just as I had done a thousand times before, and proceeded to take it out of the armoury. I'd not touched my rifle since being evacuated from the front lines. It smelt of Afghanistan, and it felt like a part of me that had been missing, but I didn't know it. I grasped it tightly as the bright sun lit up the sniper tape along the side of my weapon. The tape which I had marked each target was still in perfect condition, and so I carefully peeled off the tape and put it safely in my pocket. I raised the rifle butt into the dip of my shoulder and placed my hand on the cocking lever of the bolt action. As I cocked the bolt action back and lifted the rifle scope up to my eye, I suddenly started to tremble. Uncontrollably, like an electrical current coursing through my veins, my vision started to darken. Suddenly, an overwhelming heat came over me, and I could smell thick dust in the air. I began to hear ringing in my ears and the faint, muffled sound of someone screaming my name in the distance. My reality had completely shifted, and I was back in that place of imminent, life-threatening danger. I dropped to my knees and started to vomit while gasping for breath. My vision had gone black around the edges, and my mind's eye had completely taken over.

Flashes of scenes from Afghanistan came flooding into my head as I struggled for breath. Moments later, the lads around me quickly began to ask if I was OK. 'Yeah, I'm fine. Fuck knows what that was.' The harrowing flashes came to a stop, and they left me looking like a shock victim. I had no idea what had just happened, but I played it off as nothing to worry about and quickly headed back off to the accommodation block and I never touched my sniper rifle again.

I had experienced a flashback. A symptom of Post Traumatic Stress Disorder that would become all too familiar as time passed. Although I had no idea what PTSD was, I did know that it was taking me over, and I needed to do something about it. It was quickly becoming apparent to the people around me that something wasn't right, and the life of the party, Ted, was no longer around. I couldn't feel happiness and would often burst into tears without any explanation. I felt heavy, like a storm cloud was over me, continuously raining, and I wanted so badly to go back to war, where I thrived and felt like I now belonged. Compared to this, I felt happy out there.

Having casual anger, alcohol and violence issues was not out of the ordinary in military life, and this enabled my issues to go mostly undetected. I wanted a long career in the military and did everything I could to secure that future for myself. However, my brain had different plans that wouldn't exactly go along with the attached stigma of mental health problems at that time. I quietly began to spiral downwards into a depression, fuelled by guilt and shame with relentless images and videos playing over in my head. I'd started to humanise my targets, and once that started, well, there was no going back. There is such a thing as a moral value, and this can be attached to anything, from an object to a human being. The moral value of something like a life is usually predetermined at a young age. However, with training, this neurological standpoint can be altered. Things like bayonet training, with its screams of kill, or just referring to people as 'targets' can significantly reduce a person's moral value of life over time.

Like a burst dam, waves of remorse and sadness washed over me, and I was struggling to stay afloat. I had felt the pain of everyone I had killed and began to imagine the pain their families must have felt. I imagined the physical pain and the absolute fear that some of my targets had experienced before they died. I relived each squeeze of that trigger, over and over again, like a highlight reel being played on repeat in my head. Deafening screams would come from the inner catacombs of my mind like the souls I had taken were trapped inside my brain and screaming to get out. Slowly driving me to madness, the sounds in my mind began to distract me from reality. Like in a constant daydream, I would float through my days on autopilot, the real me hidden under layers and layers of fake smiles and jokes. Like being sat in the back of a car being driven by something else.

Intrusive thoughts would fill my day-to-day life with absolute dread as I went about normal camp life, trying to appear normal. Sudden split-second snapshots of Taliban fighters bleeding to death would be in and out of my mind all day and night. A constant soundtrack of screams and bangs would be playing along to the images. I was beginning to lose control, and I was rapidly reaching breaking point.

The storm over my head had now become a fucking cyclone, and it was crushing me. I lost friends because I kicked out at anyone who got too close or questioned my mental health. Fights were becoming a weekly occurrence as I roamed the local pubs looking for trouble. Just to be able to feel something other than sadness. My behaviour was becoming ever increasingly erratic and dangerous, and I no longer cared if I lived or died. I had fallen from a great height.

I began to look at transfer options so that I could deploy back to Afghanistan as soon as possible. I needed to be back there fighting, or I was going to completely lose my mind. Life had become boring, and camp life just consisted of nonsense lessons and pointless exercises that infuriated me for being a waste of time. My only goal was to maximise my fitness levels to prepare for the next intended phase of my career.

PTSD

Back home, life was tense, and my family were walking on eggshells so as not to set me off. However, one Sunday afternoon at home changed my life forever. Sat around the family table, about to eat dinner before leaving for camp that evening, I felt something bubbling up inside of me. Like a tsunami of rage that was growing exponentially the more I noticed it, tensing every muscle in my body and flooding me with adrenalin. That feeling of being a coiled spring was stronger than ever, and I struggled to breathe, with the raging energy trying to break its way out. A minor dispute over a spilt drink was enough to open the gateway to absolute chaos.

Blackness closed in over my eyes, and the coiled spring released. Flashes of death ripped through my mind, and my body dived across the dining table to attack. Unaware by now of what was happening, the darkness had taken over. I growled and snarled through gritted teeth as I climbed across the table like a man possessed, but my consciousness was elsewhere. Moments later, I regained consciousness. I awoke to find I was fighting with my dad on the floor. Instantly, I released him and turned around to see the look on my family's face. They had just seen a glimpse of what I had become.

I stood up, grabbed my bag, and jumped in my car to drive back to camp. 'What the fuck was that?' I thought to myself, disgusted by my actions and genuinely afraid of what was happening to me for the first time. I pondered over all the decisions I knew that I now had to make. I quickly landed on the fact that I needed to tell someone what was happening. I arrived back at my room in camp and sat on my bed the entire night with my head in my hands. I was now back in my old rifle company and under the command of a new commander, Jonsey, who was a good guy.

Monday morning came after a long sleepless night, and I knew what I had to do. I timidly knocked on the platoon office door. 'Sarge, have you got a second?' I said. 'Of course, come in. What's up, mate?' asked Jonsey. I walked in and closed the door behind me. Sat down at the desk, I started to unravel a fraction of what had been going on. Fighting back the tears, I told of the previous night's chaos at home and the mass of symptoms I was experiencing. A few minutes was all it took for Jonsey to realise that I needed help. Within minutes, he had called to make an appointment where I could speak to a visiting psychiatric nurse, who was luckily in the medical centre on camp for a few hours that day. I was terrified; I knew this wasn't going to go well, and instantly, anxiety set in.

I started to think about why the shrink was in camp and also who was already having appointments with them. It was like discovering the foundations of what I thought about the army were starting to break down. How many of these men are fucked up from this stuff? By lunchtime, everyone would know that I had gone 'head sick', and the rumours would start to fly, and it worried me. Having a mental health issue was seen as either being 'weak' or 'a blag' in an attempt to receive compensation or just get out of the Army. The stigma that was attached to such an illness was rife in the armed forces, and I knew that people would be divided in their views of me.

The Army was like a big green machine running down a railway track. If you had to get off for any reason, then that train was going to keep on running and leave you behind. Instantly, I felt like an outcast, and I hadn't even spoken to the shrink yet. I walked through the camp with my head down as I made my way into the medical centre. 'I've been sent over to see the psychiatrist thingy person,' I said as I was gestured to sit in the waiting area by the reception staff. 'Ted!' shouted a voice from one of the rooms, I jumped up and headed into the treatment room to speak with the nurse. I closed the door behind me and sat on the chair opposite the nurse's desk.

The psych nurse proceeded to explain that he'd received a call about my situation, and if I could provide some details on my symptoms, then he could try to help me. Reluctantly, I began to slowly talk through my long list of symptoms and feelings that I had been experiencing during and after the tour. Nightmares every night, crazy intrusive thoughts coming from nowhere, anger, depression, thoughts of suicide, and the list went on. After half an hour's conversation, the nurse looked up at me from his computer and said, 'I can't give you an official diagnosis, but from what you've told me, I'm quite sure that you are suffering from Post Traumatic Stress Disorder, Ted.'

It felt like someone had died or something. It felt like the carpet had been ripped out from under me, and I was plummeting to the floor. It felt like I had been pulled backwards from behind my eyes as my body was taken over by the demon. 'OK. So what does that mean?' I asked, through my thousand-yard stare. 'It means that you will more than likely be prescribed medication and therapy sessions to combat the symptoms,' the nurse replied. 'Am I going to get kicked out of the army?' I asked, with a lump in my throat. I honestly didn't think things could get any worse, but this sent any remaining strength I had left crashing to the ground. Devastated, I walked back to the accommodation block and reported back what had been said. 'They're putting me on some antidepressant medication, sarge,' I said as soon as I reached the platoon office. 'Shit, OK, mate, keep me informed. You'll get fat on them, you know though, mate,' Jonsey replied. Turns out that weight gain was just one of many effects brought on by antidepressant medication. I returned to my platoon and continued to soldier on. However, I would no longer be allowed to handle a weapon of any sort due to my awaiting diagnosis. Heartbroken and hopeless, I drank myself to blackout.

A couple of days passed, and slowly, I began to open up a little about my appointment to the lads around me. The stigma terrified me, though, and the thought of a single person there thinking I may be acting up for a payout made me sick. A few days later, I was issued with my first batch of medication, and the side effects floored me. Dizziness, fatigue, nausea, dry mouth, dilated pupils, blurred vision. The list went on, but the main issue was that these pills would knock me out cold a lot of the time. It would take a few weeks for the chemicals to make their initial way through my bloodstream and build up in my system. I couldn't think or even speak at times, and so the idea of me being able to soldier on to any degree was very unrealistic. After a while, this led to me being placed on medical leave. However, I was to report to the medical centre weekly, which luckily was only a short drive from my home to camp. I would attend appointments with therapists, doctors, and psychiatrists, but that would be the only thing I had in my diary, leaving me at home with nothing to do but to replay things over and over in my mind. All while feeling like I'd just been thrown onto the scrap heap to rot.

Not long after our arrival home from Afghanistan, we would be marched through cities that roared with pride towards us. We were idolised and called heroes. The Queen herself attended the parade where we would be issued our medals, and gallantry medals and mentions in dispatch would even be won from the tour. But that was all gone. All that remained for me were the four walls of my parents' boxroom, where the battles were far from over, and the cheers from lined streets were nothing but an echo in the distance of my mind. The fall from feeling like a superhero down to an absolute zero was gut-wrenching. Night after night, I would be frozen to my bed, paralysed by fear, as nightmarish apparitions of dead Taliban would burst into my room while I slept. The young man once known as a hero was nothing but a quivering mess.

The Taliban man shot through the throat, near the lone tree out in Afghanistan, would be my main tormentor. With his eyes and mouth stitched shut, they would be ripping to the seams as he screamed and attacked me in my nightmares. Nightly would I be dragged off into a cave, hands bound by barbed wire as I begged someone behind me to shoot the Taliban fighters dragging me away to my death, but to no effect. Nightly, I watched my friends be shot and killed as I impossibly tried to take out their killers, but to no effect. Nightmares of the most gruesome kind would wake me hourly in pools of sweat. Most nights would turn into days before I would find any sleep at all, mostly due to me feeling too vulnerable to sleep at night. Drinking wasn't helping; it only made things worse. The medication was changed and increased so often that I lost track of it all. The dosage was now so strong that at a family meal in a restaurant, I fell asleep, crashing face-first into my plate of food. The medication issued to me to help with sleep was highly addictive, and I was already on double the regular dosage. This would later lead to weeks of agonising withdrawal symptoms as I fought off my addiction to the pills. The mixture of medications was becoming unheard of. Between sleeping pills, antidepressants and anti-psychotics, the meds were equating up to fourteen pills per day.

Therapy was not working with my current therapist due to a clash, and so I was assigned a new therapist. A lovely woman named Julie. She didn't have any experience or real knowledge of the battlefield or what I had been through, which left her starting on the back foot with a seriously unwell patient. After a few short sessions, one day, I became uncontrollable as I experienced a flashback during a therapy session. The flashback was so intense that it led to me trashing the room's bookshelf in a fit of rage. I couldn't add any more guilt to my already heavy load, and I also didn't want that lovely lady to have to go home at night and think about what I had just told her. The idea of mental health was foreign to me, and I didn't understand or enjoy doing therapy. It was hard and made even harder by the apparent incompetence of the psych teams, whose training manuals looked older than me.

My care was then handed over to DCMH Donnington. This was one of the British Army's leading facilities for mental health care and therapy at the time. I was now to conduct therapy with another military therapist, who again did not have the compassion or personal traits needed to help me work through what I was going through. The new weekly appointments would also consist of a four-hour road trip, which I would have to drive alone weekly. I pushed everyone away at home and hid the severity of my illness as best as I could from my friends and family. There was no way, however, that I could hide the significant weight I had gained from the tablets' side effects. I gained six stone in weight over a very short period, and this led to its issues.

Exercise was the first thing out of everyone's mouth when it came to ways for me to feel better, but the issue was I was now overweight and unfit. The self-discipline and self-motivation that I had lived by for so many years was no longer there. I struggled just getting out of bed most days, let alone go for a fucking run. The massive amount of alcohol I was drinking had also had its effect on my weight, and now there was another problem to add to the nightmare. The mixture of so much medication and up to twenty beers in a night had resulted in a bloody stomach ulcer.

The look on my face was that of someone my friends no longer knew, but they helped me as best as they could, regardless. Dishing out cigarettes and beer to their now trembling mess of a friend. 'Go for a run,' I would hear daily from family and friends. 'It'll make you feel better,' they would say, but I had no motivation. I had never experienced anything like this in my entire life, and I simply didn't understand what was happening to me and just how quickly it was escalating.

In one of many attempts by my friends to cheer me up, they had taken me to a town carnival. Thousands of people filled the streets in what should have been a great day, but it was far from that. The huge crowds easily overwhelmed me, and I began struggling to breathe. I stopped dead in my tracks while following my friend's single file through the massive crowds. My eyes had started to go black, and I began to panic. Now alone in a huge crowd, I was about to have a flashback. I fought with my mind and struggled to keep my weak grasp on consciousness as I barged to the side of the packed street. I burst out of the crowd and into a shop doorway, as breathing became harder and harder. Tears streamed down my cheeks, and I felt my heart pumping through my chest. 'What the fuck!' I repeated over and over as I struggled to catch glimpses of reality. I thought I might be having a heart attack and crouched down to the ground with my head in my hands, getting kicked and knocked around by the passing crowds. 'Ted!' I heard my name being shouted in what sounded like the far distance. I lifted my head to try and see where the voice came from. As I looked up, there were my friends, all standing around, protecting me from the mass of people in the street. 'Come on, mate,' one of them said as they picked me up and guided me back to the car.

All I could think about was how terrifying the ordeal was and how there was nothing I could do about it. The soldier that I once was, was gone. My entire self-belief system and my self-worth were gone. My mind and the fearless war-hardened young man I used to be were gone. They were nothing but a person from another lifetime, and I could only mourn for their loss. I felt alone and hopeless, even though I was surrounded by people that cared for me.

Diving onto the floor at the sound of sudden loud bangs had happened so often as the months went by that it had become a sort of inside joke between me and my civilian friends. I had spoken to them vaguely about my time away and my struggles after my return but never opened up about everything fully. Life at home was becoming an issue, and I began to hate myself and how I was. Huge rages would terrify my parents and sister as I battled with my demons and the constant reminders of war. The stupidest things could trigger me into aggressive outbursts, such as the locking mechanism on the bathroom door. It was an old-style lock which resembled the bolt action of my rifle, and it would often send me hurtling into a flashback. News reports would show images and play sounds that would send me straight back to Afghanistan in my mind. I, even after a while, found myself looking for things to remind myself of the terrors I had witnessed. Finding reminders would flood my body with adrenalin and it would bring an overwhelming sadness that eventually became an addictive state to me. Hatred and anger fuelled me, and all I could dream of was returning to war and a bullet to the head. I felt like that was what I deserved and that an early death was inevitable.

Then, just as I felt like things could not get much worse, I saw the news. Another British soldier had been killed in Afghanistan, and it was a sniper. Daz had deployed to Afghanistan with his battalion and fell victim to an IED that had killed him.

It shook me to my core that one of the instructors from the sniper course and someone who had become a friend was now dead. The number of dead friends simply grew from that point; be it by combat or by suicide as a result of their demons, or by accident, the numbers just began to skyrocket.

Week after week at my appointments, I reported no improvement to my symptoms, only how they had worsened and that the pills were not helping. Multiple increases in dosage and multiple types of antidepressant, antipsychotic, and sleeping medications were prescribed at one time in an attempt to relieve my symptoms, to no effect, and the cycle continued.

By now, I had been away from my battalion for a few months, with only rare contact from anyone from the army. The feeling of absolute loneliness was overwhelming. Days and nights seemed to last forever, and every second of it was horrific. I couldn't bear the non-stop barrage of pain, grief and anger. The idea of suicide was becoming more and more tempting as I began to lose my fight. My doctor, a high-ranking military officer, had told me that PTSD was for life and that I could only learn to live with it. This statement would echo in my mind for many years to come as I wrestled with my mind to stay alive. My entire internal monologue was filled with hatred and disgust at myself, and the little voice at the back of my mind was growing louder. Hourly, I would be encouraged by the voice to just end it all and that I didn't deserve to be alive. I didn't deserve to be happy. I was a monster that had taken many lives, and I could no longer stand by what I had done. It just felt wrong, and so with that, I began to plan my death. It had all become too much to take. I was hurting those closest to me and putting them through their own horrific nightmare. I was all out of fight, and I still didn't understand what the fuck was happening to me. As far as I was concerned, neither did the professionals that were trying to help me. The only people that were trying to help me, I didn't trust. The only option was suicide, and I took the idea as a deserved punishment for my actions.

JUST DO IT

A short climb to a nearby cliff face on a dark winter's night was the first time I confronted the voice that had walked me all the way there to the edge. A handful of pills and a leap off the edge, and this would be done with. I stood at the edge of the cliff and let out a guttural cry of frustration. The voice inside my head pushed me every which way it could to jump off. But I stayed where I was, frozen to the spot. You see, I was fucking petrified of heights, and the thought of jumping off this giant bastard cliff, well, that was enough to scare me out of the idea just long enough to think, as ridiculous as that was. I didn't want to die, but all of the help available to me through the army wasn't helping at all, so what was I to do?

That soldier, fighting for his life daily, was still living inside of me, but the weight of it all was just too much to bear. That night was a sleepless one, and the voice in my head tormented me for being such a coward. A few days passed, and the already critical situation was about to get even worse. I sat on my bed, looking through old photographs and videos of my time in Afghanistan. It had become almost an addiction, something I would do to make myself feel something and to remember what I was capable of. But this time, remembering what I was capable of pushed me too far. I was a killer, and all I could think about was doing it again. I pulled a small black bag from underneath my fold-away bed, reached inside and grasped at my multi-tool knife. I flicked it open to reveal the sharp serrated edge, took a deep breath, and picked up my car keys from the bedside table.

Slowly, I walked quietly down the stairs of my parents' house and peered through the doorway at my mother and father sitting watching television. 'I'm just popping out for a bit, guys. I love you so much,' I said, and I quickly stepped out of the front door, got in my car, and pulled away from their house.

On the way into my village was a bridge that sat above a river. Next to the river was a small patch of gravel that was hidden away by the shadows of surrounding trees. I drove through the village, pulled my car into the darkened gravel spot, and sat opposite the church. The view was beautiful, and although I'd lived in that village all of my life, it was the first real-time I had noticed its beauty. As I sat, with my car facing the river, I replayed the same two songs on repeat, over and over again. I was ready and adamant that I had to do this. Help for this condition didn't exist. It was just an attempt using trial and error, and that wasn't good enough.

I sat in my car crying as memories from my childhood flooded my mind. I pulled the knife from my pocket. 'I'm so sorry. I'm so sorry, mate,' I cried over and over again to myself as I flicked out the serrated blade. I started to saw open my wrist with the knife, and with every slice came more and more blood. 'Keep going, you cunt!' I said to myself, over and over again through my tears and whimpers. The voice in my screaming for me not to stop. The blood soaked my jeans, and very soon, I became dizzy. I felt like I was ready to let go and let death come for me, like an old friend I had not seen for a while.

Then, suddenly, I pulled back. The last bit of fight remaining in that happy, smiling young man deep inside of me was the final chance before dying. 'What the fuck am I doing!' I shouted as I threw the knife into the passenger footwell of my car. 'No, mate! Enough is enough!' I said to myself as I looked down and assessed the injuries to my wrist. I had ripped open my left wrist with multiple deep cuts and slashes. Something needed to be done right now, or I was going to be in trouble.

I pulled off my blood-soaked hoodie and wrapped it tightly around my wrist and arm. I opened the car windows and picked up my phone. I was sure now that I did not want to die, and so I called my friends for help. Laura answered my call, unaware of my dire situation. 'Mate, I need help, are you up?' I asked. 'Yes, pop round nob head,' she replied. I hung up the phone, started my car, and quickly drove to meet Laura. Within minutes, I was outside and making my way up the steps to her house. As I walked up to the front door of her home, Laura hadn't noticed the blood covering me in the darkness. 'You OK, mate, what's up?' She asked, knowing it would be PTSD related. 'Mate, I've done something fucking stupid, and I just need some bandages and a few sugary brews, please. Don't panic.' She immediately realised the severity of the situation once she noticed the huge amount of blood soaking my clothes.

I stumbled through the door, and Laura grabbed a first aid kit out of the kitchen cupboard. I quickly bandaged myself up as Laura made a cup of tea with loads of sugar for me. After a few sugary drinks and a little talk about what had happened, I started to feel slightly better and eventually even fell asleep on the living room floor. I would, however, be caught later that night trying to sneak out of the house to finish the job.

The following day, I had an appointment with the head doctor, but there was something I needed to do before I left. I told my parents all about what had happened the night before and explained to them that I would need to pack a small hospital bag to take with me to my appointment today, just in case. I knew that what I had done would more than likely end with me being sent to the hospital for my own safety. I said my goodbyes and left for my appointment. On my arrival, it didn't take long for the doctor to notice my bandaged wrist and ask me what had happened. Busted, I told the truth and resided myself to my fate. Sure enough, the appointment ended in me being transported across the country to a facility in Peterborough Hospital's psychiatric ward.

A small wing that was used to hold British and American troops that was an annex of the main civvi psychiatric ward. Double door, after double locked door. I was walked through the hospital corridors to the ward for my first mental health assessment. The military corridor held only me and two other soldiers, who were to be discharged the following day. The first night felt like the start of a prison sentence as I heard the screams and shouts of the civilian patients down the corridor. My first few days and nights, I would be checked on every 15 minutes for 24 hours a day. My room was small and purposely designed to make it extra difficult to be able to hurt yourself. Small slats in the door would click open as the nurses checked on me through the hours. It was the first time I'd felt compassion or empathy from someone in the medical field, and it was heartwarming.

They cared for me and nursed me through the darkest few days of my life until I was capable of being alone. Heavily sedated, I would sit in front of the communal television, watching mind-numbing daytime TV with the other patients. Most of them were nonverbal and in a lot of distress, with very serious self-inflicted injuries. Kick-offs and take-downs were common, and I often found myself in trouble for trying to assist in restraining other patients to help staff. I didn't think I belonged there, and that someone else should be there in my place who needed or deserved the help more than me. Days turned into weeks, and I continued to receive care and treatment from the staff on the ward. However, the boredom and monotony that was now my day-to-day life left huge spaces of time. Time where I would be constantly under attack from my demons.

I had cut off contact with my family and friends, with only updates on my medical condition being disclosed in brief telephone calls between the nurses and my parents every so often. I didn't want any distractions and didn't want anyone to worry about me. I needed to get better, and to do that, I needed to be alone. Except for one thing that I missed dearly. My guitar.

One Saturday morning, the day started with the usual chaperoned breakfast, followed by the usual morning talk with the patients about the day's activities. One of the nurses took me to one side after the meeting and asked if I would like to go into town for a couple of hours, obviously escorted by him. I had been on the ward for the longest time out of all the patients at this point and had not left the ward once. The idea that I could go out and maybe buy a cheap guitar filled me with excitement and even made me smile for the first time in months. 'I'd love to, mate, yes, please, thank you,' I said, and quickly grabbed my things, and we headed off to the bus stop together. The short journey from the hospital to the town centre gave me a chance to breathe and a chance to peer through the windows of the bus, day-to-day life just continuing to go on without me.

We headed straight to the local music shop, and for the first time in a long time, I felt alive. I looked through the huge range of guitars hanging on the walls of the shop. The smell of old chord learning books took my mind straight back to being a child. Sneaking up to my dad's wardrobe and quietly playing on his guitar while flicking through old songbooks. On the bottom row of guitars was a black Fender acoustic guitar, and it was perfect. Five minutes later, I was walking out of the door, ready to head back to the ward. A simple trip into town was enough to riddle me with anxiety, though, and over the next few days, I only ever left my room for meals. I sat day and night, playing my new guitar and writing songs. My lyrics helped me to cope and became an outlet for things I couldn't say out loud. I didn't realise at the time, but I was making the first steps towards a better life. Two more weeks went by, and I had written an entire album of songs. Years later, I would find myself listening back to the words of wisdom written by my former self to aid in my recovery. I had now been at the facility for a month, and one day, out of the blue, I was told I would be getting transferred to another hospital. This new psychiatric hospital would be slightly closer to home and have more help available to assist in my recovery.

The moving day quickly came, and I stood at the doorway of my ward, saying heartfelt goodbyes to the staff as I waited for my transport to take me away. The driver turned up, and he had been sent from my regiment to take me to the new hospital. It was the first and last contact I would have with anybody from the battalion for a very long time. I felt forgotten and angry, and the journey was a quiet one, but soon enough, I'd arrived at my next stop. I walked up to the doors of the new facility and was met by the members of the team who would be responsible for my care. Sadness had overrun me at this point, and I simply had nothing left in me, I felt broken.

My anger built up inside my head as I thought about not hearing from anyone outside of the hospital. Days of silence followed as I became seriously unwell. I'd started to hear and see things that simply were not there. Machine guns, explosions and people screaming my name would echo around my mind while steadily increasing in volume until I reached a breaking point. I would find myself vibrating with adrenaline and frustration as my condition worsened and the deepest, darkest parts of my PTSD set in. In my peripheral vision, I had begun to notice something, but I couldn't turn fast enough to see what it was. Anytime I tried to look, the figure would move out of sight. I thought I was losing my mind completely, and it terrified me. I eventually began to see the young man I had shot in the throat, and that haunted my dreams. My nightmares had somehow made their way into my perceived reality.

One afternoon, I sat alone in the communal area, with my hood up and head on a table, in quiet tears. My mind was tormenting me, and I couldn't take it anymore. I stood up, walked over to a crafts table, picked up a pencil and a pencil sharpener, and quickly walked off to my room down the corridor. Walking through my door, I burst into floods of tears and began to punch the walls as I lost control. The sheer weight of my sadness was quite literally enough to drop me to my knees.

The sharpener lay on the floor next to the pencil as I paused, staring at them through blurred, teary eyes. I knew why I'd taken the sharpener, and as I stared at it on the floor, I lifted my foot and stamped down on it, shattering the plastic casing across the floor. I lifted my foot to reveal the broken pieces of plastic and the small shiny blade that lay among them. I picked up the blade, my hands bloodied from my split-open knuckles. I sat on my metal framed bed and placed the quivering blade against my only just healing wrist. My anger overflowed through my body as I began to apply pressure to the easily broken skin.

I began to cry uncontrollably. Again, I did not want to die, and I frustratedly threw the blade to the floor and began to trash my room like a child throwing a tantrum. It was the only thing that seemed to release some pressure from my head, and as I began to calm down, I picked up the blade. Again. I couldn't kill myself; I just couldn't, and so I walked out of my room and down the corridor to the duty nurse's office. I reluctantly knocked on the office door and explained what I had just attempted to do, and apologised for the damage I had caused to my room.

That day in the office, I met Lucy, a warm-hearted, caring soul who had been designated as the go-to nurse for all the military personnel at the facility. There were only three of us there, including me, but we were all high risk, and all needed seriously intense care. Lucy sat and spoke with me in a small office room. I sat there crying as the hood of my Afghanistan tour hoodie covered my face. I was supposed to be a 'tough guy sniper', not a crying mess, but I just couldn't stop. She spoke with me at length about what I'd been through and what I was currently experiencing. Quickly, she managed to bring down my walls slightly and got an insight into who I was. A happy, caring young man who had been trapped inside a cage and was being tortured. I had forgotten all about my happy old self. Most of the lads had forgotten about their old selves, though.

Lucy cleaned up the injuries to my knuckles and asked if I would like to go for a walk just out around the hospital grounds. I half agreed, and we walked around the hospital, talking deeply about my condition and my feelings.

The following morning, after breakfast, I woke to the sound of a knock on my door. It was Lucy and her massive smile peering through the glass. The medication was still wiping me out in the mornings, and I slept a lot of the time during the day. 'Come on, I've got something for you,' Lucy said. She asked how I was feeling, and I told her I felt even worse than the day before.

A night filled with nightmares had left me on edge and coiled like a pissed-off spring, ready to blow at the slightest thing. Lucy walked off down the corridor and simply gestured for me to follow. She walked down the corridor and through a small side door that led out to the smoking area. As I walked through the smoking door, Lucy stood there with a plastic bag in her hand.

The area was mostly grass and enclosed by high wooden slat fences. Lucy reached into the plastic bag and pulled out a pair of boxing gloves. Lucy had been out into town that morning before coming to work and had bought and paid for the gloves with her own money, all in an attempt to help me. 'Put them on,' she said, as I stood with a confused look on my face, but did as I was told. 'Right, now punch that fence. Punch it until it breaks, and then move on to the next one,' Lucy said, 'What? I can't do that!' I replied. 'Just do it, Ted, do it until you can't do it anymore. Don't worry; they can be replaced, but you need to get this anger out of you right now. So punch it!' I turned and attacked the fence panel with furious anger. I punched through the wooden panels repeatedly until I was exhausted and could punch no more.

It helped, and for the first time in a long time, I was able to slow my mind down just enough to have a much-needed moment of peace. I went on to explain to Lucy how taking my shots in Afghanistan had felt like throwing a huge killer punch in some crazy way that could stretch over to the enemy. Over and over in my mind, I would hear the shots being fired and see the catastrophic injuries caused by them in flashes like in old films. Constantly throughout the day and night, they would play over and over in my mind. So many emotions were attached to them that it simply overwhelmed me. However, right now, they were quiet for the first time in a long time.

IT'S TIME TO START TALKING

Just a few days after punching the fences, I began talking therapy in an outpatient ward at the old hospital, I would meet with a new civilian therapist named Julie. We would have two sessions weekly of Cognitive Behavioural Therapy – CBT – which was a talking-based therapy that was hoped to relieve some of the symptoms I was experiencing and, over time, process those memories and reduce their effects on me.

Time at the psych ward went by slowly. Days were filled with colouring books, bingo, eating hospital food, and now therapy, all on repeat. A month into my new ward, an appointment was called to discuss my progress with consultants in the field. I had now been under the care of the NHS psychiatric facilities for two months in total, and Christmas was fast approaching. The appointment was to assess my condition and, most importantly, my risk to myself or others. Twenty minutes sat with the specialists, and it was deemed that I was in a good enough condition to be sent home, and I was to continue my rehabilitation and therapy within HM Armed Forces.

Two weeks after my discharge from the hospital, I was readmitted after another attempt at taking my own life. The words 'PTSD is for life' spoken by the doctor ran through my mind constantly. I had a life sentence of torture and pain, and I couldn't bear it. Nurse Lucy was sad to see me back on the ward and in even worse condition than my previous stay. I wanted it all to just stop. The pain, the anger, the guilt, the shame, they all had their agendas to inflict hurt on me. My mind was giving up on me, and I was in free fall. This time at the hospital, there was no therapy. Just care and compassion, as the staff on the ward did everything they could to help me through each day. For another month, I would stay there on the ward before being in a stable enough condition to return home. Taking with me some strength that I'd managed to muster from the nurse's encouragement.

A few short weeks after my return home from hospital, I was called into camp. There was still the overhanging dread of what would happen to my career or if I was to have one at all after all this. It only took four men, who'd never met me before, to decide that the Army was no longer a viable career for me and that I was now medically unfit for service.

The men in suits made up their report, however, only shining a light on a small percentage of my issues. That was enough to warrant me medically discharged from service, bringing the end of my career, my dreams, and my livelihood. The medical report expected me to fully recover from my PTSD within the next five years, which confused me as I had already been told I would have the condition for life.

Weeks went by after the medical review, and then I was instructed to make my final visit to camp before my discharge was complete. I would need to hand in any issued kit and clothing, have some hearing, eyesight, and dental tests done, and then collect my military records.

I said my goodbyes to the small rear party in the camp that I knew, handed in my ID card, and I walked out of the giant barbed wire gates for the last time.

My care had now been passed over to a sparsely funded department of the NHS called NHS Veterans Wales, which operated out of unused hospital rooms around the country. I soon received a letter informing me that I had an appointment at my local hospital for my first therapy session with a man called Doug.

Broken and in a state of desperation, I attended my first appointment with the new service and my new therapist. Doug was one of the therapists who worked with Welsh veterans to help improve their lives and regain control. He warmly welcomed me into the office and began to explain who he was and what types of therapy could be available to me.

Instantly, I felt at ease with Doug, and after just a few sessions, I was able to open up to him more than any other therapist in the past. Therapy was hard, and it involved a lot of homework that I would need to complete. This, however, would send me into fits of rage at home, and it was just not realistic at the time. I couldn't even read or write without the sounds in my head screaming at me. Weeks went by of Doug breaking down the barriers and teaching me various techniques that I could use to calm myself when I was beginning to become irritated.

I talked through most of the things that had happened in Afghanistan, and Doug just listened. This wasn't his first rodeo, he knew that I had a lot built up inside that needed to come out. I told Doug that the images in my head would sometimes become too powerful and simply take control. The more they came, the more I would fight against them. Pushing them away was the only thing I thought I could do. However, it was exhausting. Every aspect of having PTSD was exhausting, and that is what made it such a dangerous condition.

One day, Doug asked me to picture a purple elephant. 'Just picture it in your mind's eye, Ted, and once you can see it, I want you to keep talking to me.' I did as I was told, and sure enough, I was able to picture a purple elephant right there in my mind. Doug started to talk about one of the events in Afghanistan that was causing me some trouble. Then he stopped and said, 'Stop thinking about that purple elephant now, Ted, stop seeing it in your head . . . I said to stop thinking about the purple elephant, Ted, now!' I laughed, 'I can't mate, it's just fucking there!' And with that, Doug smiled.

The 'purple elephant' example gave an outside observation of how one's mind works. If somebody is told not to think about a purple elephant, the individual, by nature, will picture a purple elephant in their mind's eye. The 'purple elephant' is such a ridiculously specific thing that it will stick to your mind like gum to a shoe. The more you try not to think about a purple elephant, the more you see it, and the more you try to push it away. PTSD memories, and also other memories with a negative attachment, can easily act in the same way as the elephant. There are many reasons for someone to push away these images or thoughts, but in doing so, they only intensify. Without knowing what the individual is doing, we fight harder against the images and, in turn, strengthen the problem at its source.

Dough explained this theory to me, and instantly, it made sense. 'Fucking hell, that's some good therapy stuff that, mate,' I laughed, elated by the fact I had just received the best piece of help from a therapist to date. Sessions would only last for an hour, and so there was never enough time to move on to the next thing, but for the very first time, I was coming around to the idea of therapy. The usual alpha male, tough guy opinion on talking therapy was that it was a crock of shit. I could no longer see it that way, after all, therapy had just thrown me a very much-needed safety rope.

TRUST THE PROCESS

I began to see an improvement as the weeks went by and found some of the techniques Doug had shown me very useful. I was by no means better, but I did now possess some tools I could use to fight back the right way, and that gave me hope.

The nightmares were relentless every night, and the flashbacks were still powerful enough to drop me to the floor. After either a nightmare or a flashback, I would struggle to reconnect to reality and could often go days in a sort of trance state, barely able to speak.

Doug knew that I needed help with coping with such events, it was the first in many steps towards recovery. 'OK, Ted, today I want to go through something called a grounding technique. These are for when you are experiencing that confusion between realities or to possibly stop an oncoming flashback.' I sat up straight and eagerly awaited Doug's next words. This was exactly what I needed, and I could not wait to get started.

'OK, sit in your chair I want you to close your eyes and just relax. I want you to listen carefully and tell me what you can hear.' I sat and soon started to pick up various sounds. The clock on the wall was ticking, and a fan was blowing over in the corner. Doug had turned on a tap very slightly over at the hand sanitation sink so I could hear the dripping. I could hear birds singing outside of the open window behind me. 'OK, I want you to feel the chair you are sitting on. With your hands, feel the different textures and materials. You are here!' Doug went on to explain how grounding myself in times of struggle would help me to clear my mind and regain my touch with reality.

The nightmares were making it impossible for me to sleep, and even fearful of falling asleep due to the absolute terror they brought to me each night. I spoke about my nightmares in depth during the therapy sessions, but every session would start with me saying I've had no sleep and that the nightmares are killing me.

In one session, Doug explained to me why I was having these nightmares and why they were so invasive and overpowering. He told me to imagine that I have an office clerk living inside my brain. Surrounded by never-ending filling cabinets and paperwork, the clerk rushes through the night, sorting and collating all of the day's data entries and memories and putting them away into the relevant cabinets.

However, some of the memories which need to be processed and filled away are just too terrifying for my clerk to handle. These bits of traumatic paperwork are left to float around the office as they please, the clerk too afraid to try and file them away again. They cause havoc, and while I slept, my dramatic paperwork was running wild. The only way to stop the nightmares was to help the clerk via CBT and Eye Movement Desensitisation and Reprocessing – EMDR – therapy. Cognitive behavioural therapy was a way in which I could learn to adapt to the way my brain was working and thinking. therapy was a way to disconnect the feelings or emotions from the memories of these traumatic events. Neither of which made sense to me at the time. For now, though, there was still work to be done on my coping techniques. These were my new weapons.

I was starting to open up more and more to Doug about my day-to-day struggles with things like crowds, bangs, and various other things that would set me off. One session ended with me talking about my confidence and just how much anxiety I was living with. I had always been bright and bubbly to most people, but I was just too exhausted to pretend anymore. My anxiety was causing plenty of its own effects, but one in particular was my off-the-scale sweating. The anxiety and side effects of my medication were causing me to have huge sweat patches under my armpits, and it became a real issue for me. Not only was I now overweight, but I also had a pair of sweat patches to go with my new fucking belly.

'Shall we go for a quick brew in the hospital cafe today, Ted?' said Doug one morning at the start of a session. 'Yeah, OK, mate,' I replied, happy to get some caffeine in me. We walked over to the busy cafe, got our coffees, and sat down at a small table in the centre of the crowded seating area. Sat down, I was uncomfortable as Doug began to talk. 'I need to pop to the toilet, will you be OK here for a minute on your own?' I did not like the idea one bit, but I needed to push myself, and so I agreed. 'Try not to sit there on your phone; it's a bad coping mechanism for social anxiety. Just sit and relax, have a look around.' And with that, Doug left.

'Fuck me, this place is way too busy. And I'm sat right in the fucking middle of it all. Shit, I need to get out of here,' I thought to myself as I sat alone, not looking at my phone like a good fucking boy. It was a difficult exercise to do, just sit there. This was starting to feel like a set-up. Suddenly, Doug was back, and after making his way through the busty cafeteria, he started to take off his coat. He reached both his hands high in the air as he removed his jumper to reveal a light blue shirt. Doug hadn't needed to go to the toilet at all; it was all a ruse. He had gone to the bathroom and soaked his fucking armpits with water from the tap. He made no effort to hide his giant 'sweat patches' or even pay any notice to them as he sat down with his hands behind his head with it all on show.

'Have a look around, Ted, does anyone seem to be looking at me or my armpits?' Doug asked, 'No, nobody gives a shit.' I looked around and just saw people going about their own lives with their own problems. 'You see, it doesn't matter if you have sweat patches. It's not the big thing you have made it out to be, Ted.' I just sat there leaning back in my chair and put it all into perspective, but the main thing I took away from that was that Doug would go out of his way to help me.

RIGHT, THAT'S ENOUGH

The voice in my head would repeat the words spoken by the army doctor, that my condition was for life. Over and over, it would repeat in my mind as I thought about therapy. I had been going for quite some time now, and with that, I began to think. Maybe this was as good as it gets, and that therapy just meant that you go and learn these techniques, and then you just get on with it.

I started to think about how I didn't deserve the help or even the time of Doug, who was now an increasingly important part of my recovery. 'Someone else needs this time more than me,' I would say to myself again and again as I began to feel guilty for taking up therapy spaces. Over the next few sessions, I started to convince Doug that I was fine now, and I appreciated the help, but it was time for me to leave therapy. My symptoms were reducing, and my medication was working. I needed to try to get on with my life, or at least try to build a new one.

Time went by slowly as I struggled to find work, and I started to rely heavily on alcohol again. It didn't take long for the dark, heavy cloud of depression to descend over my life once more as I drank until I passed out most nights.

A few weeks before my three-month stay in hospital, I was out drinking in my local town. I drank as much as I could, as fast as I could, and more often than not, I would do it alone. Most nights would end in violence or tears, and this night, in particular, was no different.

I sat in the early hours of the morning on the floor outside of my usual drinking hole. A rough pub, where I could easily get into trouble if I wished it so. A drunken mess with tears pouring down my face, I sat on the dirty, wet floor, smoking. Out of nowhere, a figure approached and sat down next to me. She was beautiful and had the most infectious laugh that I couldn't help but cheer up. It was a foreign feeling, but this girl had something special about her. She sat with me on the cold, wet floor as I poured my heart out to this total stranger.

She listened, but not like anyone else had listened. She didn't listen for gory details or anything like that. She didn't care or even stop to think about the tales I told her of my battles overseas; she seemed to just see the boy. She saw it all from a whole new perspective, one of empathy. The boy inside of me, who was so full of light at one time, but now sat crying in the street.

It didn't take long for this young woman to get me up on my feet and safely to the taxi rank down the road, where I could find my way home before morning broke. That night, I slept with a small piece of light inside of me, brought out by a brief encounter with a stranger.

Months went by for me after I stopped therapy with Doug, but it didn't feel like living; nothing excited me anymore. Life was dull, and I needed some excitement or at least something to look forward to.

A group of my friends from home were planning a backpacking trip through Southeast Asia, and this was exactly what I needed. I needed adventure, and I wanted to see the world in a different light. Thailand was just the place to start, and very quickly after our arrival, it started to have an effect on me. Seeing the Buddhist culture and the Thai people's way of life was like flicking a switch in my mind.

I saw a peaceful life and true happiness, and it was infectious. By the end of the trip, it was clear to me that this was something I wanted to do. The slow pace of life and the way people who even had nothing were happy brought me to a realisation. There were so many people worse off than me, and they seemed to live a happy life, so I could too. The beaches and jungles seemed to breathe life into my soul, and my friends made an effort in every town we visited to get me up on stage to perform to the locals, including a performance to 10,000 people at a New Year's Eve street party. I had lost my identity, but performing on stage seemed to be the only real place I could forget about my problems and just be me.

Music had become my main interest while at home, and I had started to perform in pubs wherever I could, performing the songs I had written while in hospital multiple times a week. I was starting to find myself again, but I was still fighting with the demons in my mind. After a while of playing my songs around the UK, I managed to sign a record deal with a small label in London. I toured the UK playing shows every night, but I was wearing a mask of smiles. The reality was it was way more overwhelming than I could have imagined. I released another album, but soon after its release, I knew things still were not right. I wanted to pursue my love of music, and I had done since a very young age. I had always wanted to be a professional musician, but my mental health was getting in the way. I'd often play to a small gathering of troops back in camp, and it brought me great joy to be able to unite people with music. It was supposed to bring joy and emotion, but all I had to offer was overwhelming sadness. I was stuck in a loop, and the way things were heading didn't look too good. Something huge had to change, and fast.

CHANGE IS SCARY

A few of the troops that had served with me had now left the Army, and they were on their own adventures all over the world, and I was inspired by them. Deep down, I knew that I was capable of doing it myself, but I was terrified that I would become seriously unwell while travelling abroad.

Getting so way outside of my comfort zone was the only way I could see myself being able to reclaim my life and try to move on from my past.

Jamie was a good mate from the reconnaissance platoon and also my first rifle company back in the battalion. Either by luck or by fate, I came to hear of Jamie's imminent departure to Australia. I had always wanted to visit Australia and wasted no time in getting in touch with my old pal.

A quick phone call between us and I had booked my flights and my visa. This was it, the change that needed to happen.

Flying around my friend's kitchen with my laptop and passport in hand, I shouted, 'I'm going to Australia, lads!' My friends sat around the room and looked up at me with a confused look. 'I've just booked my flight, and I'm going to Australia for a couple of years, boys.'

I was buzzing with excitement, and for the first time in a long time, I had my spark back. I had always been the kind of person to just go with the flow of things, and this was the first sign of my old self that I'd missed so much, and it made me smile.

The past few months since my departure from therapy had been tough, and I had seen a shift in my views on the recovery potential and process. The traditional methods of therapy that I had tried and the drugs that had been prescribed to me had little to no positive effect. The grounding techniques Doug had taught me helped me to recover from flashbacks or panic attacks but by no means were they a cure for any of it.

The mass amounts of medication prescribed to me had been a living nightmare, with a huge list of side effects and withdrawal symptoms.

I even suffered a lasting injury from the medication in the form of a stomach ulcer. The pain from the ulcer was sometimes excruciating and felt like another weight added to my already overburdened shoulders.

Nightmares still ripped me from my sleep at night, and flashbacks would devastate me for days on end. Even while on unimaginable doses of medication, I would still be powerless against them, as well as incurring the harsh side effects of the pills that were supposed to be helping me.

I decided that I was going to stop taking the medication, and after consulting with my GP, I proceeded to come off the antidepressants, antipsychotics and sleeping pills that had sucked the life out of me. They seemed to be doing more harm than good, and so the daunting withdrawal process began. No sleep for days, lying in cold sweat-soaked sheets, shivering like an addict. Searching through draws, looking for just one more sleeping pill. This went on for weeks, and it left me exhausted and empty. My nervous system felt jittery, and I could hardly think straight, but there was no time to sit around feeling sorry for myself. The medication was gone, and with it, any help that it may have been providing.

Deep down, I knew that I still needed help, but I was still a stubborn-minded bloke with a stubborn-minded outlook. Drugs are bad, therapy is for wimps, and all you need is to lock it all away in the back of your mind. Forget about the past, and just move on with your life. I thought that if I could distract myself, then it would all just go away with time.

I had to find some peace from somewhere, though, or I was going to stay the angry time bomb that I was forever. I began to research alternative methods for recovery and the world of holistic healing, and soon, I began to practice the art of meditation.

I started by listening to guided meditation recordings, which would take me on journeys through my mind's eye, which would leave a feeling of happiness. It took some time to reach a level of competence with meditation, but persistence and a desire to heal kept me going.

My departure to Australia was fast approaching, and the pressure was on me to be in a good mental head space for my adventure.

Deep breathing exercises would boost my mood in the mornings or whenever I needed them. Simply taking a few minutes to take in as much oxygen as possible would make a noticeable difference in my mood.

Meditation, yoga, and breathing work were now the foundation of my personal recovery routine and paired with the excitement of my upcoming trip across the world, I started to feel partly normal again.

I began to gain confidence, and now and then, little glimpses of that happy young man would shine through. One specific symptom of my PTSD, however, was still extremely powerful, and it could feed on me at will: the nightmares.

Haunting images and videos of real situations would ravage my mind as I slept. Night terrors would be so frightening and disturbing that I would be too scared to sleep. The pills couldn't stop them, and so far, neither could the meditation, no matter how much I dedicated to it. There was another option that was not commonly available, nor was it legal, but results from testing over in America were looking very promising.

HOLISTIC HEALING

The medical use of cannabis was coming into an exciting new age, as was the science behind it. I would read reports of American soldiers who had used cannabis in their recovery from PTSD and the medical reports that supported them. I was desperate for something that worked, even if it was just temporary.

I had nothing to lose; after all, I wasn't in the Army anymore, so drug testing wasn't an issue. The law, however, did worry me and the implications of being caught by the police in possession of cannabis or the judgement that would be made on me by others. I quickly realised, though, that nothing was more important to me than me. I needed to get better, and everything else I had tried had failed me.

So I got hold of some, and the first night I smoked that plant, I felt an instant release. That coiled spring feeling that was so overwhelming at times seemed to just loosen immediately. I felt like it all just drifted away for a moment, and there was peace. The sounds in my mind were gone, and the anger had softened.

That night, I slept the best I had done in years and woke the following morning having slept straight through the entire night. There had been no nightmares or freakouts in the night, just sleep. I couldn't believe it, and the following night, I did the same thing. Rather than take a pill made up of all kinds of different chemicals, I would smoke this flower that was incomparable in effect. The second night held the same result of no nightmares, or at least none that woke me or that I could remember. 'This could be the answer,' I thought to myself, 'Or at least part of it.'

The meditation and breathing exercises, coupled with smoking the cannabis, had revitalised my mind and given me a much-needed mental rest from the torment.

I continued to research medical cannabis and how it worked its magic on the brain. I pushed the boundaries of my meditations and learned how I could go deeper into my mind, using cannabis as a shield from the emotions that would arise. My mind's eye grew stronger, and my connection to the universe and its powers grew with it.

Meditation is all about relaxation and just going with the flow of your mind. Deep, calming breaths, to begin with, flood the body with oxygen, followed by controlled breaths. On closing your eyes, your mind's eye takes over. In a meditative state, I would simply observe the images that would appear. Good or bad, I would let the images guide me through my mind. I was just at the tip of it all, but I could see the power that meditation had, and it had already taken me into deep trace-like states on multiple regular occasions.

This is where I could begin to heal myself or learn from what I was shown. I saw how my anger was affecting everyone around me, and it was the first thing that needed to be addressed.

Waking up in a bad mood was the way most days started for me, and after a while, I would become angry about just being angry. This was where I found the cannabis useful. Seconds after lighting up, the anger would just drift away, and my tense muscles would relax just enough for me to let go for a moment.

The rare opportunity for a moment's peace was a welcome one. However, I did not want to rely on cannabis every day just to get through. Instead, I would opt for meditation and breathing exercises more often than smoking a spliff.

Night-time however, was a different story and was, without a doubt, the worst time of day for me. As darkness fell, I would notice the hyperactivity in my brain increase. My hypervigilance would skyrocket, picking out every sound or movement as if it were Taliban at the door. I didn't feel safe and would often spend the entire night not making a sound and just listening for an attack.

Though I was trying my hardest to battle my PTSD with meditation and mindfulness, the night-time hours were a different beast. Anxiety levels would go through the roof, leaving me shaking like a shell shock casualty depicted in an old war movie. Pure fear would course through my veins, and the only thing I knew to do was to get angry. 'Get angry, and you'll get through this,' I would often say to myself. If anger and aggression could get me through on a battlefield, then surely it could do the same for me now.

The cycle continued on a daily rotation in my head, but right now, I had to be OK, I had no other choice. Time was very much ticking for me and Jay as our departure date arrived.

Goodbyes were never easy, but it was something that our families were used to by now. Jay's visa arrived just in time as we packed our bags and slept at our family homes for the last time in who knows how long.

All I could think about was my mental health and what might happen to it once I arrived in Australia.

SYDNEY

The flight to Australia was long, and although very excited, I was apprehensive about my mental health and whether or not I had made a big mistake by running to the other side of the world. But Jay was a very good friend, and a very good human being who would be there for me every step of the way.

We landed in Sydney and had previously arranged to stay with my friend Laura, who had emigrated there some years earlier. We stayed a few days at her place and made the most of our time in Sydney while basing ourselves out of Bondi Beach. Soon, though it was time for us to head off to our next destination, and hopefully the chance of some much-needed work. Before leaving Sydney, though, there was something I needed to do.

'I need to get a guitar, and then I might be able to make some money with it,' I said to Jay. A quick bus ride into the city and, we found ourselves in some kind of guitar megastore. Wall to wall, floor to ceiling, nothing but guitars. The store felt to me like I had just stepped off the world for a moment, and I thought about absolutely nothing but music.

Up high, there on the third shelf of guitars, hung a shimmering black Acoustic that seemed to stand out from all the rest. Similar to the one I had bought during my stay at the hospital, I knew I had to have it.

The store worker took the guitar down off the wall and handed it over to me. 'Yep, that'll do me just fine,' I said after having a quick play. We had been in the shop for only ten minutes, and I had just spent half of my savings on a guitar.

We had to find jobs and quickly to save enough money to be able to survive for a while.

We made a plan, and luckily Jay knew a guy who might be able to help us find work. Jay had a Canadian friend called Jason who had been in Australia for a while. He was working in a remote town only a few hours away. Me and Jay said our goodbyes to Laura and jumped on the train to head out on to our next chapter.

Jason met with us, and we both moved into the same backpackers' hostel. Sure enough, two days later, we had found work.

We had found a job working on the outskirts of town. On a tree farm, pulling small trees from the ground behind a tractor. It was backbreaking work, but we were certainly used to a bit of that.

Pretty soon, though, we found ourselves on the lookout for better jobs with better pay, so we placed an advertisement in the local papers with an agency and, the very same day, got a call.

'Hello, is that the two Pommie squaddie lads?' shouted a deep Australian accent down my phone. 'Yeah, that's us, mate, how can we help you?' I replied.

The phone signal was bad enough, let alone having to translate an outback bush accent. 'I need two lads to come and live on the farm for landmarking,' I heard the man say. 'Yeah, no problem, mate, we can do it all, don't you worry,' I said back to the crackling voice down the phone. 'Send me your address, and we'll be there tomorrow morning.' I turned to Jay, and we jumped about with excitement at the opportunity.

We needed to complete 88 days of agricultural work in order to receive our second-year visa to stay in the country, and the job on the farm would allow us to do that. Also, we were going to receive free accommodation and a decent wage. The job was too good to miss, but there was a problem.

'Hey, how the fuck are we going to get all the way out there?' Jay said. 'Shit! We need a car!' I replied, and we fell about the place laughing, stood in the middle of the local town's tiny music shop, of course.

This time, however, it was Jay that was spending the money. He had an interest in music himself, and he bought himself a guitar there and then. 'OK, let's go,' Jay said. 'This is going to be so good. Just three months of us practising guitar together,' I replied. 'Right then, we need to find a car!'

We decided we would run down the huge main street that ran through the town and look out for cars for sale. It took no longer than two miles to find the perfect car, and after a swift phone call, we became the new owners of a golden Toyota Camry.

We drove our new car back to the hostel and said our goodbyes to our new friends. Jason, our Canadian friend, had completed his farm work days and had already moved on to live in Brisbane.

THE FARM

Two hours on the road, and we had seen maybe a hundred cars. This place was way out there, and we had some way to go yet. Kangaroos lined the roads as I turned into a pub car park to check the map.

We had arrived at our destination town, but we still had a while to go until we reached the farm where we'd be working. Me and Jay drove up the main road that split the town in half.

It was an old farming town north of Melbourne, and all the old buildings looked like something out of a Western movie. 'Fucking hell, what have we gotten ourselves into here then?' laughed Jay. 'What is landmarking anyway?' he asked.

'I have no idea, mate, suppose we'll just be walking around marking out where this fella's land is. Spray stuff on the floor, maybe, or maybe it's a fencing job. Fuck knows?' I replied.

'Yeah, that sounds about right, I guess we'll find out soon enough,' Jay said.

The main street consisted of a couple of restaurants, pubs, a grocery store, and a few other shops. It looked like time had stood still.

'Turn right here, mate and then we just follow this lane for 15 kilometres,' said Jay. I drove down the narrow country road, and the further I drove, the smaller the road became until we came across a gate.

'That's it there, I think Ted,' said Jay, and he jumped out of the car to open the huge white gates. 'How the fuck do you open these bloody things then?' He shouted as he pushed and pulled the gate back and forth. 'Try that button over there,' I shouted back.

Suddenly, we could see a white truck quickly heading towards us from the farmhouse. 'Hello, lads, follow me,' shouted an Australian voice from the car window.

I drove up the dirt track road, rolling behind the truck until it pulled up next to a barn. We jumped out of the car and walked over to meet our new boss.

'Hey, fellas, I'm Bill. Nice to meet you,' said the farmer, who towered above us. A huge, shovel-handed sheep farmer stood in front of us with a smile from ear to ear.

Instantly, I, who was feeling pretty anxious about the whole situation, felt relaxed. Very quickly, we could both tell that our new boss was going to be a good one, and we had, without question, landed on our feet.

'Quickly, grab a motorbike from the shed and follow me lads, we need to go check on some sheep in a paddock just a few fields over there. You can both ride, can't you, fellas?'

Me and Jay looked at each other and quickly replied, 'Yeah, of course.' Jay had a bike when he was younger, and even though it had been a while, he got straight into it.

I, on the other hand, had not spent much time on a motorbike at all and had about 60 seconds to learn from Jay how to ride the bloody thing. Luckily for me, it was only a quick 20-minute round trip on the bikes, and then it was time to see our new, free, accommodation.

'This is it, gents. It's not much, but I'm sure you'll make it home. I lived in here myself when I was younger,' said Bill, the farmer, as he stood outside of a small wooden cottage on stilts that sat a few hundred metres away from the main farm buildings.

He showed us around the tiny abode, which had one bedroom, a bathroom run on rainwater, a living room and a kitchen. 'I'll let you settle in for the evening and see you in the morning,' said Bill, and we set about bringing in our bags.

'Hey, Jay,' I said. 'I think when I spoke to Bill on the phone, he might have said lamb marking and not landmarking you know mate.'

'Yeah, mate, I think he said that too you idiot,' Jay joked, but we still had no idea what lamb marking was. That evening, we cooked up some food and took in the beautiful scenery around us. Wild birds sitting along phone lines and kangaroos hopping around just mere feet away from our cabin.

Me and jay sat at the kitchen table as the sun dipped below the horizon, bathing everything in a dark orange glow. 'Fuck! Ted, don't move for a second. There's a fucking redback spider just abseiling down off your chair, mate,' and he began to giggle.

I looked slowly under my seat to see the spider just inches from my bare leg, and it would be fair to say I nearly shit my shorts. I quickly pulled my leg away and jumped across the room. 'Fuck me man, day fucking one like!' I laughed. Jay grabbed a cup, and I grabbed a plate, and we quickly threw the spider out of the door.

The sun had now set, and the dark skies provided the perfect conditions for some of the most incredible stars that I had ever seen. As clear as day, I could see the Milky Way just sitting there, and we both stood on the decking that surrounded our new cabin home in absolute amazement.

The following morning, we woke bright and early with the sun and headed over to the farmhouse to start our first day. 'Morning, fellas, you ready to go? Jump on a two-wheeler and follow me,' said Bill as he stuffed the last of his breakfast into his mouth and pulled away on his own supercharged motocross bike. 'Nice easy day today, boys. We'll head out a few kilometres and just bring back a few sheep to the shed,' he shouted.

Jay and I still had no idea what our actual job was, but by now, it was very clear that sheep would be playing a big part in it. 'How many sheep do you have, Bill?' asked Jay. 'Seventeen thousand sheep on seventy-five thousand acres,' Bill replied with a grin on his face.

Pretty soon, Bill pulled off the dirt road and into a huge, waterlogged paddock. 'Right, fellas, take the dog with you and go fetch them sheep over there.' Me and Jay looked at each other, and without a word, we both knew exactly what each other was thinking, 'Fuck.'

The farm dog had ridden up on the back of Bill's bike, and it ran over and jumped straight on the back of Jay's motorbike. 'If you get stuck, just follow the dog!' Bill shouted as he pulled away down the road and left us to it. 'Right then, let's go heard some fucking sheep!' I shouted, and we set off through the puddles and ditches at the start of the field.

Neither of us had ever worked with sheep before or even on a farm, but we weren't going to let that stop us. It had only been a few minutes into our ride across the paddock, and Jay's muscle memory for motocross bikes had come right back. As he scrambled across the mud and water, Jay stopped for a moment to see if he could spot any sheep up ahead. 'Ted, they're down the far end, mate!' He shouted as he turned his head to look back at me. The little green Kawasaki bike I had been riding was lying at the edge of a ditch, but I was nowhere to be seen. Instantly, Jay kicked his bike into gear and made his way over to the messed-up bike. Just as he pulled up to the bike, I popped my head up from below the ditch, absolutely caked in mud and soaked to the bone.

'Fucking bastard thing, man!' I shouted as I brushed myself down. I had lost control of my back tyre as it skipped across the muddy ground and then I went straight over the handlebars and into the ditch. Luckily, there were no significant injuries, but it had knocked my confidence for a moment. We laughed until tears rolled down our cheeks, but we quickly had to snap back to business.

The sheep in the distance were on the move, and with a wave of dirt flying through the air we raced off after them. It took quite some time to gather all the sheep together, but the dog knew exactly what to do and showed us just how to do it. Like steering a hovercraft, Jay and I bounced from side to side at the rear of the flock, and soon enough, they all started to head in the right direction.

Half an hour later, the sheep were back at the shed, although we had no idea what happened in the shed. This was, after all, our first day on the job, but that was no excuse. 'Right, fellas, push them up this way, and we'll get to splitting them up,' said Bill, who was doing most of the work.

Males, females and their lambs were split up and pushed off into separate pens. The larger sheep would be getting sheared in the next few weeks and were soon released into the closest paddock. The lambs, however, needed to go through the lamb marking process.

This was it, me and Jay were about to find out what we had actually been hired to do. A small temporary pen had been made up for the lambs, and each side of the square had a metal cradle-looking contraption.

Giant hand shears, bottles of medication with syringes, ear tags and hole punchers lay on the grass around the pen, which was filled with lambs. The lambs were only a few weeks old, and for them to have the best chance at life, some procedures needed to be conducted on them.

Blowfly was a serious threat to the livestock out in Australia, and if a sheep became 'fly struck,' then its chances of staying alive were very slim indeed. The flies would burrow into the wool around the lamb's tails and lay their maggots, which in turn would eat their way out of their living host.

To protect against such issues, Jay and I would need to catch the lambs and place them in the cradles. Once locked in, we would have to place tags in both ears, inject them with medication, remove their tails using the hand shears, and also the skin surrounding the animal's anus. It was not a nice job, and both of us were quite taken back by the whole process.

The lamb marking work went on for weeks, and we gritted our teeth and just got through it. Thinking about the time coming when we would have completed 88 days of work on the farm and be able to finally move on to a new adventure.

Weeks of hard work had left us gagging for a beer, and so, for the first time, we headed off into town. 'Lads, just be careful when you go for beers. One of the pubs in town is known for being a bit of a punch-up pub, and the local Aussie footy lads are always giving people a bit of a kickin,' said Bill. 'Just be careful.'

A few beers were all it took to have me and Jay making friends with the locals and explaining what we were doing in such a small, remote town. The only British lads in the town tended to stick out like a sore thumb, and we thought we might as well go and see what this rough pub was all about.

I pushed open the saloon-style doors, and everyone at the bar turned to see who was coming in. We bounced over to the bar and had no intention of just having a quiet pint and going unnoticed. We would, after all, be staying in the town for the next three months, so we thought it best to just be ourselves and see how it goes.

Several beers in, and the intrigued local nutcases and hard men were making themselves known to us. Some were standing just a little too close, and some were as loud and intimidating as they could be, but we were unaffected. We continued to drink our beers, stood right at the centre of the bar, and then we were approached.

'What the fuck are you doing in here?', growled one of the local blokes as he grabbed me by the arm. I turned slowly to look at the drunk man. 'Take your fucking hand off my arm, mate, or you'll lose it,' I said calmly and quietly to my antagoniser, who was trying to start a fight. Jay stood just behind me, ready to snap into action.

The young man was one of the town's so called hard nuts, and the whole bar stopped to see what was about to happen. The Aussie tough guy let go of my arm and began to poke me in the chest and ribs with his fingers 'What are you going to do about it? He continued to taunt me, and it looked like a punch-up was brewing.

'You're getting on my fucking tits now, you cunt!' I shouted as I took hold of the man's wrist and tweaked it slightly, just enough to send pain shooting up his arm. 'Listen to me dickhead; you are trying it on with the wrong blokes. You see, you want a little pub brawl to get your kicks. Whereas, me and him prefer to get our kicks in a fucking war zone. Pathetic little cunt, now go sit down and drink your beer like a good lad.'

That bloodthirsty demon had awoken inside of me, and I was not messing about. I felt my eyes sink back into my head, and a glaze covered them like an overlay of all the things I had seen in war. Jay quickly stepped in and managed to calm me before I lost my temper for real.

The locals stood around watching as a tormentor of their town was reduced to the likes of a boy, with just words and a thousand-yard stare. The man did as he was told and sat quietly with his beer at a nearby table while we continued to drink, our good mood unaffected by the whole situation.

It turned out that Bill was right to warn us about the pub, but never did we think that later that very night, me and Jay would be invited to a huge house party by the local football team, who we had been warned about, and that we would soon become known by most people in the town and make some great friends there.

Day-to-day life on the farm was never the same, and as the weeks and months went by, we both had plenty to do. Putting up kilometres of fencing was a big job that me and Jay would enjoy. Heading out on the quad bikes or trucks to far away fields would give us ample opportunity to get to see some of the wildlife in the outback.

Snakes, spiders, birds, bats, lizards, and kangaroos had all become a part of our day-to-day, but one day in particular, while putting up a fence, Jay spotted something on the ground. 'That's a massive nest! What the fuck is that for?' He said. I ran over to take a closer look at the strange-looking nest. A huge purple egg sat in the middle of the giant nest, and neither Jay nor myself could fathom what on earth it was. That was until we remembered Bill telling us about the wild emu that would sometimes visit the farm.

Suddenly, we heard something in the distance, and as we moved slowly away from the nest and its purple egg, there it was. A huge emu was making its way towards us, and we both jumped on the floor and raised our arms in the air. Bill had told us that if we made an emu neck shape with our arm and hand, that usually the emu would come over to investigate, and it did just that. We couldn't believe what we were experiencing as the giant wild bird came close enough to almost touch.

Close encounters with the wildlife were a pretty common occurrence by now, but one of them would be more frightening than enjoyable. Apart from the odd poisonous snake appearing out of nowhere, nothing really posed a threat to us. It was only really the very unlikely event of a kangaroo attacking one of us that concerned us.

Some of the adult kangaroos in the area were almost 7 feet tall and built out of nothing but pure muscle and giant claws. One day, while out collecting sheep from a far-out paddock, I was riding my motorbike quickly down a muddy, slippery dirt path. Jay had already made it through the sketchy section of ground without problem, but my back wheel wobbled from side to side as I struggled to keep upright. A fence ran along the righthand side of the track, and a thick bush lined the left.

I managed to speed up slightly and gain more control of the bike just as something caught my eye up ahead in the bushes. A kangaroo head bobbed up and down in the distance as I hurtled towards it at over 30 kilometres an hour. All of a sudden, the huge adult kangaroo revealed itself and bounced straight over the bushes and onto the dirt track directly in front of me. The gigantic animal bounced its way straight towards me, and there was nothing I could do. The bike was going too fast on the slippery surface to manoeuvre out of the way, and it looked like a collision was imminent.

I lowered my head and braced for impact, keeping my eyes on the kangaroo. Just at the very last moment, the kangaroo loaded its weight onto its powerful back legs and sprang itself into the air. I could only watch in amazement as the creature flew up and straight over my fucking head and just carried on about its day.

COUNTING DOWN THE DAYS

Work on the farm was tough, but the toughest part was yet to come. Shearing sheep in Australia had been named as one of the top ten hardest jobs in the world, and it was to be the next challenge for us. Taking control of adult sheep and rams and shaving off their wool was no easy feat, and neither was processing the tonnes of wool afterwards.

Both of us had worked hard on the farm, and as a thank-you, Bill's father-in-law offered us both the chance to fly his private aeroplane. To drive from one end of the farm to the other on the road would take around an hour, and so the use of a plane to observe the land was more than useful.

'So meet me on the airfield at seven tomorrow morning, lads and we can fly out to Deny airport and grab some breakfast,' said Bill's father in-law, 'Absolutely, will do,' I replied.

'As if we are going to fly a plane,' laughed Jay in disbelief as we walked back into our cabin.

We had come from a culture of drinking a lot of alcohol, and so the excitement of our upcoming flight was too much to take, and we headed straight out to town for a few Friday night beers. We had both become rather popular with the locals by now, and most people knew we were a good addition to any party, even though we did have a reputation for eating any food that may be around at people's houses.

Two other British backpackers had been employed at another farm in the town, and they were out for a drink themselves. Me and Jay introduced ourselves and made the pair feel welcome in the somewhat intimidating town.

A few beers quickly turned into a full drinking session just as the pub pulled out the karaoke machine and we sang into the early hours.

Birds sang, and the sun seemed to have melted me to a cream leather couch. I could barely open my eyes to make out a tiled floor, which I did not recognise. My vomit-covered shirt lay on the floor as I slowly turned my head to look for Jay. 'What the fuck. Where am I?' I said to myself as I tried to gather myself. 'Oh shit! The plane!' I shouted, and

I stood up as best as I could. Suddenly, the front door of what looked like a bungalow opened.

'Bro! You missed it!' Jay burst through the doorway with a huge smile on his face. 'Mate, I just flew a fucking plane! I tried to wake you up, but you were completely passed out.' I had slept through the whole thing. Jay had just about made it to the airfield on time and, indeed flew over the town that morning. I was gutted to have missed the experience, but the whole story was so funny that we couldn't stop laughing.

Our time working at the farm was coming to an end, and we had become almost a part of the family. The children from the farm went to a private boarding school in Melbourne, but they had come home for the school holidays. They got to know me and Jay, as did the grandparents. We even spent some time zeroing rifles and teaching the son how to shoot. We had created the best of memories there and were sorry to say goodbye but also ready for our next destination.

We planned to make the 13-hour drive to Brisbane and meet up with Jason and the rest of the gang as soon as our 88 days were up.

The final week of work was a pretty easy one, and we had plenty of chance to explore the area on the motorbikes. One day, we spotted a small building way out at the edge of the land, and we just had to go and take a closer look.

A wooden shack with a rusted roof barely stood up in the middle of a small field. It looked like nobody had been there in decades. Huge cobwebs covered the derelict building, and dead animals littered the floor.

Through the doorway, deep in the darkness, I spotted what looked like a wooden chest surrounded by boxes. 'We have to go in and have a look, don't we?' I said, as Jay wasted no time and bounded through the door. 'Fucking hell Ted! Look at this!' He shouted. I looked over Jay's shoulder as he started to pull bottles from the chest. 'What the fuck is that?' I shouted. 'It's wine! It's vintage wine, mate! And there's port over there, too!' Jay said, tongue in cheek. 'We're taking that,' I said, and we wasted no time grabbing the boxes of booze and stashing them for later. That evening, we drove back to the area in our car and packed the crates away safely in the boot. That night, after a little bit of research, we estimated the bottles to be worth thousands of dollars, and some of the bottles were over a hundred years old.

Friday came, and it was our 88th day working on the farm. We had completed our required agricultural work, and now we would be able to stay in the country for two years. Everything was coming together, and both myself and Jay were very ready for a change of scenery.

My mental health had been OK, but I was still struggling with it all internally. I was doing a pretty good job of not thinking about it and had plenty to keep me occupied, but the nightmares and intrusive thoughts were still very much a part of my day to day life.

An old friend from the army had been in touch with us, and he was going to be in Brisbane for a few days. Me and Jay had previously planned to leave for Brisbane on the Saturday morning, but when Bill told us to finish early that Friday afternoon, well, we couldn't resist.

It took us no more than 20 minutes to pack our entire lives into our trusty gold Toyota Camry and hit the road. The weather had been pretty bad for a few days, with several inches of rain falling, causing some flooding, and the long dirt road from the farm was now mostly under water.

'Let's just fucking go for it,' I said from behind the wheel. 'Yep. Do it!' Jay replied, and I hit the accelerator. The car bounced from side to side on the slippery track until eventually landing in the deep tracks made by the trucks that had carved out the path. Finally, we reached the main road. Our car was completely covered from top to bottom in mud, but nothing was stopping us now. We quickly rinsed off the car and waved goodbye to the town we had called home for the past three months.

It felt good to leave, but the next 13-hour drive was going to be a tough one. An hour into the drive came a huge electrical storm, leaving trees scattered across roads and mass floods. We swerved around fallen tree limbs in the road and splashed through the deepest of flood puddles, with rain bouncing off the car roof all of the way.

A quick bit of sleep in a shop carpark, and we were straight back at it, and just as we reached the mountains behind Brisbane, the sun came out.

BRISBANE

As me and Jay drove into the outskirts of the city, we both had a smile from ear to ear. I could not believe for a moment that this was really my life and that this was not a dream. I was so grateful to be alive, and as the warm sun touched my skin, I took a moment to appreciate just how far I had come.

Since I had first decided to move out to Australia, I had begun to work hard on losing some of those pounds of fat I had put on due to my medication. Fitness was always the first piece of advice anybody would give me, and now I had the self-motivation I needed to act. I began to train at least twice a day, usually a cycle and a run. I learnt about nutrition and its effects on the body and the mind.

The endorphins released while running would liberate me from bad moods, and the fact that I was starting to look like myself again was extremely rewarding. There was no way I wanted to start my new chapter in life as any kind of old version of myself. I was determined to reclaim my life and fight for the life that I wanted.

Jay had the body of a granite statue, and that also inspired me to lose weight. Jay helped me with exercise routines and encouraged me when things were hard. He was the perfect person for me to learn from, in more ways than one.

As the city buildings began to tower over the our heads, we reached our destination. Our first stop was at a Brisbane backpackers' hostel where we would be reunited with our old brother-in-arms, Dez.

Dez had recently moved out to Australia and had secured himself a well-paid job on an outback farm. He had been a recognised rugby player back in the UK, and the farm's local side needed some boosting, so Dez was hired to come and do his thing on the pitch.

It had been years since we had all seen each other, and the instant we were reunited, it was like it had been just days. The bond that is made between troops that go to war together is as strong as a family bond, and these three brothers wasted no time in heading to our new home and getting on the beers.

Our new home for the foreseeable future was just on the edge of the city, and as we pulled up to the address, we could hardly believe our eyes. The house was huge and surrounded by very nice houses indeed.

The million-dollar property had been bought for its ideal location and size, with a future plan to demolish the house and build a multi-storey car park. It had a basement room that looked like something from a frat party film, huge rooms, and it was the ideal place to throw a party.

Including me and Jay, the house would be occupied by up to ten people at a time. As we climbed the stairs to the front door, we were greeted with the biggest cheers and smiles that we could have ever hoped for. Jay knew some of the guys living there, but I only knew Jason, the Canadian, from back at the workers' hostel three months prior.

Instantly, we were welcomed into the house family that was made up of people from all over the world, and instantly, we were handed a cold beer. The group had been awaiting our arrival, excited to show us what Brisbane had to offer.

Jay and myself were exhausted from the drive there, but we put in a valiant effort with the late-night party. While staying on the farm, we had started to play some songs together. One hot day, Jay had left his acoustic guitar under the air-conditioning unit, and it had broken it. So I suggested getting a cajon, a box drum, which he could play beats along to my guitar and vocals.

That first night, as the nightclubs closed and the party headed home, me and Jay started to play. As we finished playing a few songs, we both had a bright idea. The party was dying, and the booze was gone, but we had a trick up our sleeve.

We discreetly made our way down out of the house and to the boot of our car. 'Who wants some wine then?' we shouted as we burst back into the party, carrying the cases of vintage wine we had relieved from the farm shack. The night ended in a blackout, and the following morning, we realised that we had drank the lot, thousands of dollars of wine gone in just one night.

After a week or so of enjoying ourselves, it was time to find work. Carl was one of the guys living at the house from Birmingham, and he was just about to leave his job working at a backpackers hostel in the city. He arranged for me to replace him in his role, driving the hostel minibus and doing other various duties around the place. It was a great job, and I enjoyed working there. Meeting people from all over the world and all walks of life seemed to put my own life into perspective.

The past few years had been hard, to say the least, but seeing backpackers younger than myself, I could not help but see some of my youth as wasted. I knew that my past had shaped me, but there was a lot of resentment towards my old military life.

It seemed that my demons were starting to awaken yet again, and the inside of my mind started to become a dark place. As close as I had now become to everyone in the house, I could not express how I was feeling on the inside.

It felt like my bubble was about to burst, and the thought terrified me. The nightmares and flashbacks I had endured for so many years had started to slowly creep back into my life, and my anxiety began to build.

'How is this happening when I'm quite literally living in paradise?' I thought to myself, and soon I knew that I had to act otherwise, my situation would only worsen.

One thing had stayed with me throughout my struggles, and that was music. I had continued to write songs and keep my skills sharp while on the farm and now in my own bedroom at the house.

One of the bars in the city happened to be looking for an entertainer to play a couple of hours on a Wednesday night, and seeing as me and the other lads spent a lot of time there, it was an easy enough decision to let me take the spot.

Nerves filled me, but so did excitement at the thought of performing live again. Even though it was just a Wednesday night slot, I and the lads all spread the word like wildfire. Brits that were staying at the city hostels were all excited to be entertained by one of their own for a change, and a buzz grew about town.

I had played in a couple of open mic nights in the city prior to my own full gig, and I seemed to have impressed the small audiences and had started to receive messages about private party bookings.

Finally, the Wednesday evening arrived, and as the lads had a few beers at home before heading out, I practised my setlist. 'It's time to go mate. Are you ready?' said Jay. 'Yes, bro, let's do this thing,' I replied, and the whole group piled into a couple of cabs and we headed for the city.

We arrived at the bar, and everyone grabbed a piece of equipment and headed up the steps. The door was crowded with people smoking around it as we made our way into the bar. 'Oh my God! Ted, look at that!' shouted one of the lads.

I turned the corner and saw people standing shoulder to shoulder, from front to back. The place was filled with backpackers drinking beers and waiting for the show.

The owner of the bar could not believe what was happening. Two hundred people had filled his usually quiet bar on a Wednesday night, and he instantly booked me for every Wednesday from that point on.

A huge network of backpackers was the perfect market for me to tap into, and the huge efforts made by me and my new friends had paid off. The night went perfectly, and I had now secured himself some regular gigs.

A few weeks went by, and the Wednesday gigs had now turned into Wednesday, Friday and Sunday gigs. Promoters in the city had started to book me for shows, and word began to spread further than just the city of Brisbane.

Playing music regularly seemed to do just the trick with my mental health, and the bubbling symptoms that I was experiencing were starting to die down. I even managed to sign with a small record label on the Gold Coast, and life felt good once more.

As the months flew by, the bond between me, Jay, and everyone related to the house had reached the closest of levels. A small group of young men where ego had no part.

It allowed me to almost soften my war-hardened exterior and learn from each of the people around me. Meditation and mindfulness played a big part in my life still, as did cannabis. The word-of-mouth knowledge about other substances which could be used for recovery and healing was easily spread between the likes of backpackers and hippies, and it was something that I was keen to explore.

GOODBYE AUSTRALIA

As people's work visas came to an end, the group living at the house decided to plan our next adventure. Me and Jay had been in Australia for a year when we booked our flights back to the UK. The plan was to pop home for a little while before heading off on our travels again.

The memories that had been made in Australia so far had been incredible, and the experience had been life-changing. The next planned trip was to Canada, starting out in Jason's town. The group, which consisted of me, Jay, Carl, Jason, Tim, and Grace, would head down the West Coast of America and into Central America, but first, we had to get home.

Me and Jay set off on our homeward journey by first taking a flight from Brisbane up north to Cairnes. From there, we would fly to the Philippines. The flight up to the Northern Territory of Australia was only short. The flight from there to Manila was longer, but there was free beer. Hooray.

We were always good fun, and the more free beer we consumed, the more fun our flight became. The night flight was a quiet one, with there being more empty seats than filled ones. The aircrew found us entertaining and were happy to give us a list of places where we could party in Manila that night.

We had a 16-hour wait in the city for our flight back to the UK, and both myself and Jay intended to make the most of it. We landed in the Philippines and set about finding somewhere to store away our baggage. A small office room was open, and in our drunken state, we hid our luggage in there and caught a taxi into the city.

We went from bar to bar, and ended up in a nightclub deep within the city's party district. The last memory we both had was sitting on a giant swing, gliding overhead at the nightclub, and then yet another blackout. We awoke inside a taxi cab as it pulled up outside of the airport terminal. The aircrew from our flight had been in the nightclub and paid for the taxi to take us back to the airport so we didn't miss our flight home.

Me and Jay tried our best to sober up as we walked through the airport and snuck into the office room to get our bags. An airport security guard caught us in the act, and us drunken pair of idiots set off running.

We ran through the crowds and finally made it to the security check line. As we stood quietly in the queue, I received a tap on the shoulder. I looked back to see a group of security guards standing behind me. We couldn't help but burst out laughing, and by some stroke of luck, the whole chase through the airport was seen as a bit of fun and the security guards began to laugh. The lead guard simply said, 'Money for the boys.'

After paying the guards and making our way through security, we fell asleep outside of a closed bakery shop.

Jay and myself spent upwards of 40 hours getting from Australia to Wales, and we already had plans for our return. While out in Brisbane, we had started to busk out on the city streets, and we had now got a full set list of songs which we could play together.

The following day after our arrival back in the UK, we had been booked to perform at a local music festival. It was a great chance to catch up with family and friends and also put the word out that we were looking for more gigs while we were home.

It didn't take long though, for my mental health to take a big drop, and I could feel my old, furious ways creeping back in. Anger was one of my biggest problems, and I would still have daily intrusive thoughts about my time in Afghanistan.

The memories and pictures in my mind began to get stronger, and I again knew that I had to do something in order to help myself.

PTSD could have this hold over me, like a black hole of sadness was constantly sucking me in, and it was powerful. It was powerful enough that just the thought of going back to how I used to be frightened the life out of me. I was desperate to escape the misery that followed me and then came a phone call from Jay.

'Hey, bro! How are things?' I was candid in my reply, 'Fucking shit, mate. Can we just fuck off already?' Being home just reminded me of sad times, and being in the spots where I had tried to commit suicide just a few years earlier was very triggering.

'Well, Carl is in Portugal now, in a place called Lagos. I've been there before and had a great time, shall we just go there?' Jay said with a cheeky tone in his voice. 'Yep, let's fucking do it. I'll find flights now!' I said excitedly.

I had been staying with my friend Harry, who had always kept an eye on how I was doing and helped however he could. I was lucky to have him.

A few days later, and me and Jay were landing in Lisbon. We boarded a graffiti-covered train in a quaint little train station and headed down to the south-eastern coast.

PORTUGAL

A hot destination for surfers, the small town was filled with Australians and we wasted no time in getting to know everyone around town. Carl had secured himself a bed at a hostel and, with it, some work, but he was lucky.

The town was filled with backpackers looking for work, and there were nowhere near enough jobs to go around. Me and Jay had managed to save a little money, and we had a bunk bed in a small hostel, so for now, we weren't worried.

We were happy to be back in the hot sunshine, and living a life of freedom. The town was widely known as a little vortex that would tend to keep people there for longer than they had planned, and for me, this could not have been more perfect. We had plans later in the year, but for now we were just drifting in the wind.

The party was non-stop, and the people were amazing. Everyone was constantly smiling and talking to each other like they had known each other for years. This was absolutely the place that I needed to be.

Me and Jay began searching for work after a few days, but things were not looking good. All of the positions in town had been filled, and every bed in town was now booked up for months. Money was starting to run low, and so we made a plan.

We had taken our instruments with us, and so the obvious choice was for us to start busking in the town square. It had worked in Brisbane and at home, so why not here?

Our plan, however, was quickly put to a stop. The square was filled with buskers of all types, and in order to busk there, we would need a permit. The news was devastating, but we wasted no time that morning heading down to the local council offices and applying for a licence.

Jay and I walked out of the air-conditioned offices and out onto the scorching hot street. 'Two weeks! What the fuck are we going to do?' I said. Our permit would take two weeks to be processed, and so we faced the very daunting fact that we could well be looking at sleeping on the beach. 'We've still got two days left in our hostel, but after that we are fucked!' Jay replied.

It wasn't uncommon for us to face trials and tribulations while travelling abroad, but we always tried to stay positive about our situation. Our time in the army had shown us some of the hardest times in our lives, and so nothing would really ever appear too difficult compared to that.

'Let's go for an afternoon beer and see if we can make a plan,' I said, and we walked through the winding cobbled streets of the small town until we heard music.

A small bar had a guy singing in the back, and we thought this would be the best place to have a beer and make our plan. The bar was dark and mostly painted black, with a small stage at the end of the bar that sat roughly five feet high.

We both sat at the bar and got talking to the staff there for a couple of minutes just as the singer announced he was taking a break. 'Would anyone like to come up on stage and play for ten minutes while I have a break?' said the singer as he climbed down from the stage.

'Yeah, I'll have a crack mate,' I shouted instantaneously. I knew that all I needed was the chance to prove my skills, and I'd be able to get us work. I jumped up onto the stage took hold of the acoustic guitar, and started to play.

The bar was quiet, but I played like my life depended on it, and by the end of my first song, a small crowd had gathered to watch me. People stopped at the doorway to the bar as they passed on the street, and I released all my stresses through the music.

The bar was renowned for looking after its live musicians, and a bucket was always passed around the bar for every act to collect tips. The bucket came back to me, and it was peppered with coins and notes from the crowd which had now left.

'You guys want a whisky?' said the barman to the two new faces in town. 'Love one,' we replied as I wiped the sweat from my face. We sat, and as we lifted our glasses, the barman said, 'So, do you want a job then?'

I smiled, 'Absolutely, mate. We're actually a duo; he plays a box that he sits on.' We all sat at the bar and finalised on us playing on a Monday afternoon and a Thursday afternoon. It was perfect but by no means enough money to live on. Even if we made a fortune busking, there was still the problem of no rooms being available in town whatsoever.

In true British squaddie style, we thought that was a problem for tomorrow. After all, we had just landed some work, so it was time to celebrate. We spent the night meeting people at the bar and spreading the word about our upcoming afternoon gigs.

The next morning, we spent on the beach, while flicking through local job advertisements, I noticed one that stood out to me. An old guest house in the next town along was looking for two workers to help around the place. The 300-year-old building and its gardens needed some looking after, and the job came with free food and accommodation.

We wasted no time in getting in touch with the owner, and after a quick call, we had the job. We would start the following morning, and so we packed our things and prepared to leave. The next town was only a 15-minute bus ride along the coast, but the town itself was much quieter.

An old fishing village, Burgau was made up of a few small restaurants and bars, quaint white villas, and a couple of shops. As the bus pulled into town, I spotted the guest house just up the road.

Huge rusty gates and a long dusty driveway lined with dying grape vines seemed slightly daunting as we made our way towards the house. White paint flaked from the walls, and the surrounding gardens had all died, leaving the place looking like a scary movie set.

Fifteen-foot high wooden barn doors sat to the left-hand side of the main building, and there was music playing from just inside. 'Hello,' shouted Jay as a figure moved towards the door from the darkness.

'Hi, I'm Ted, and this is Jay. We're here for the two maintenance job vacancies,' I said, as the man in front of me just stood there with a confused look on his face.

'My name's Sue. I've got no idea what you're talking about, lads sorry, it must be something to do with Sally. She owns the place but never tells me anything, I'll take you to her.'

Sue was a Scottish man in his late fifties with shoulder-length grey hair and bohemian style clothing. As a young teenager, he had left home and travelled the world. He told us about his life, from living in Hawaii to being a transient living on freight trains. He was certainly an interesting man, and he had worked at the guest house for several years in a life of mostly solitude.

'Sally, I have two ex-soldier musicians here that tell me you have hired them,' said Sue as he guided us through the corridors, which seemed like a timeless cavern that had decades of books and trinkets, all stacked on top of each other as high as the ceilings.

Sat in a comfortably worn-out arm chair, deep in a darkened room, sat a frizzy white-haired lady well into her eighties. 'Yes, come in!' she shouted sharply. 'Hello, Sue, can you sort out room two before they arrive for me, please. Lads come here, let's have a look at you.'

I approached the slightly concerning woman, quickly followed by Jay as she started to list off the jobs that needed doing around the place and what other work she wanted us to do.

'You can stay in the old chicken shed at the bottom of the garden, and I will buy food for you both to eat. Head around the side there and drop your bags off on your bed. Then come and meet me in the kitchen.'

We walked out of the house and off towards our new home. The building was old and steeped in pirate history and stories of smugglers' tunnels. It was filled with character but in need of some work, but that added to its character.

We walked through the lengthy back garden and came across the lone chicken shed. A tin roof building that had a small doorway and a window which backed onto a dried-out field. On entering the tiny building, we saw a single bed, a chair, and a small sofa.

We both laughed at our dire situation, but we couldn't help but feel lucky as if something was always looking out for us. Suddenly, a loud noise came from the window. 'What the fuck!' Jay shouted as a horse's head poked through the small open window.

It was by no means a hotel room, but it was free. Plus, we had free food and got to work outside in the sun. We dropped our bags on the 'bed' and made the short walk back up to the kitchen.

The guesthouse was ran completely by Sally and Sue. It never had more than five or six guests, but the extra helping hands would be more than useful. The kitchen looked like that of a hoarder, and there wasn't much in the way of food. Some out-of-date Portuguese tarts and a bag of leeks seemed to be the only things edible, apart from the 'guests' fridge.

It was clear that things were not to be as advertised, but we didn't mind. We would get the bus into town each day to busk or play gigs, and pretty soon we had created a little life for ourselves in Portugal and were usually right in the centre of a party.

By day, we would tend to the garden, and we found it a great way to express our creativity as we landscaped the grounds and encouraged them back to life. We even made friends with the horse behind the chicken shed.

The afternoon gigs had become a bit of a weekly highlight for the travelling workers in the town and the other musicians that played the bars, and me and Jay soon began to play the busier nights.

We would pack out the bar and the street outside as we played for hours on the tiny stage, and the tip bucket would never disappoint. Often, it would be passed back to us filled with money and drugs, and one night we even received a pound of bacon as a tip from one of the local chefs. We were having the time of our lives, but the time of our lives came with some serious fucking hangovers.

One hungover morning after playing our busiest gig yet, me and Jay were awoken in our chicken shed by a bang on the door. 'Wake up you two. I need you in the kitchen,' shouted Sally, who never came down to the chicken shed before.

A couple of minutes later, she was banging on the door again. 'I have some guests going out on a yacht today, and I need you to make them a packed lunch. 'What the fuck. No way. I feel like I'm dying,' I mumbled to Jay. 'Yeah, we'll be there now,' Jay shouted back to Sally.

We got up and quickly started to get dressed as we heard Sally shout, 'And bring your instruments!' We made it up to the kitchen and started to prepare a packed lunch for the trip. The idea of being on a yacht with this hangover while making some leek-based treats was too much for my stomach to handle, and I ran outside to throw up.

Lunch was eventually all packed, we got into Sally's car, and off we went. A quick stop at the grocery store to pick up a cooked chicken, and we headed to the port in Lagos. We pulled into the carpark just as we were greeted by a small group of guests which Sally had known for many years.

Jay and myself found the yacht captain, and loaded our stuff aboard the very impressive-looking vessel. Sally, who had now got a following of around fifteen people, walked around the corner and made her way aboard.

We still had no idea what was going on, and we quickly chugged a couple of beers to help with the hangover. The yacht set sail around the southern coast of Portugal, and pretty soon Sally had us entertaining the passengers, who turned out to be the family of the legendary Billy Idol.

After a quick stop in a bay for a swim, and a cheeky go of another yachts jet ski, we played all the way back to port. I could not believe the life that I was living, and it started to feel like all of my troubles were now in the past.

Determined that positivity would pave the way and attract positive things in the process. More and more of these positive events were happening, and it seemed like luck was always on my side. Life was a happy experience again, and soon, it would be time to leave for the next adventure.

MARGE

Now back in the UK, me, Jay, and Carl had all met on the train heading to the airport. After an early morning start and a few hours of sleeping on the floor at the airport, we were boarding the plane to Calgary.

The flight went quickly as we grew in excitement for our next adventure, and could not wait for it to begin. At Calgary airport, waiting for our arrival, were Jason's mother Sarah, and his aunty, Jodie, who had both emigrated to Canada from Wales many years ago.

They welcomed us with huge smiles and a giant Welsh flag, and they instantly treated us like family. We all jumped in the car, and headed out on the long drive to Jodie's house, where we would be staying for a few days.

Tim and Grace, the two Australians, were staying at Sarah's house, but they had not arrived in the country just yet. Me, Jay and Carl arrived at Jodie's house and could not believe our eyes.

It was huge, like something from a movie, and it was in the most beautiful location on a hilltop near some forestry that overlooked the town below.

A couple of days went by, eating the most amazing home cooked meals and desserts, and being cared for like the closest of family. A few days later and the whole crew were back together, and it was time for phase two of our epic journey.

Me, Jay, Carl, Jason, Grace and Tim had a mammoth task ahead of us; we needed to find a motorhome that would last the trip. It needed to be large enough for six people to live in for the next few months and also be capable of making the 20,000-kilometre meandering drive down to Central America.

We went to look at a few potential vehicles over the coming few days, and then we found her. A 1980s Ford motorhome called Marge. The previous owners had named the vehicle Marge after their first motorhome named Homer had burnt in an accident.

It was perfect for us young adventurers, a double bed above the driver's cockpit, a double bed at the back, a table that folded into a bed, a small bathroom and a kitchenette. Only five bed spaces meant that each night, the crew would all rotate sleeping positions while one person slept on the floor.

We drove in convoy back to Jodie and her husband Nick's house, and just as we reached the outskirts of town, we pulled over to see the Aurora Borealis shining brightly over our heads like a good omen.

After a big party with Jason's family and friends, it was time to load up Marge, do our final checks, and say our goodbyes to some of the nicest people we could have ever hoped to meet.

A quick group photograph in front of Marge, and it was time to hit the road off into the unknown. We were heading up through the Rocky Mountains for a spot of hiking and to check out the famous stunning blue waters of Lake Moraine and Lake Louise, which had just received their first dusting of snow. The views were truly breathtaking, and I could not help but feel a connection to the nature that surrounded me.

After a few weeks of travelling through Canada, we travelled south. Down the West Coast of America we drove, stopping in the towns and cities, Me and Jay would busk on the streets to make money. The adventures we experienced were the things that dreams are made of, and what most people would only ever see in movies.

We climbed a volcano; we spent Halloween in Hollywood, we drove through wildfire, we climbed the mountains of Yosemite to break through the thick smoke. We witnessed the migrations of dolphins and whales in the Pacific Ocean, we stood with the largest tree on earth, we played jazz with strangers on stage, and were invited to a secret speakeasy jazz club, we played live on the national news on Thanksgiving. We took part in the world pillow-fighting championships. We swam with dolphins, fed wild birds from our hands, dumpster dived for our food, and the list goes on and on.

We made it all the way down to San Diego, and camped up in the carpark of a small fun fair that was right up next to the beach. Surrounded by giant palm trees, we stayed a few weeks in the carpark before heading into Mexico.

Travelling through Mexico, we encountered many dangers, but nothing was going to deter us.

Every day brought new challenges and experiences, from corrupt police interactions and gangs to small villages and their occupants, who were always surprised to see a young group of backpackers in a giant motorhome. Mountain roads with certain-death drops just inches away, waterfalls that seemed to go forever, ancient ruins and the stories of their civilisations.

We had arranged to park Marge outside of a backpackers hostel on the southern coast of Mexico, at a surfing town called Puerto Escondido. After a nine-hour drive through the mountains, we finally reached our destination. We ran an electricity cable from Marge across the road and plugged it into the hostel.

Puerto Escondido was not a well-known destination for travellers at the time, and it was quiet most of the time. The buildings were basic and usually made from corrugated tin and breeze blocks. The roads were made of sand, and nobody ever wore shoes.

We spent our days drinking cold beers and surfing most of the time and would usually have a pack of local dogs that would go with us wherever we went and would look after our belongings on the beach. We had no plans on leaving anytime soon, and we stayed right where we were for weeks. Life was slow-paced, and we enjoyed every minute of it like it was the last minute of our lives. Eventually, though, our savings began to run out, and as careful as we had been to live as cheaply as possible, the inevitable was that me and Jay would have to return to the UK.

BACK TO THE UK

While travelling, I had noticed a decline in my mental health but never really spoke about it too much with anybody. I had everything I could ever need to distract me from my inner thoughts, and the idea of having poor mental health whilst exploring paradise was just far too miserable of a thought to bear.

My time travelling the world had shown me so many amazing things, but the main thing I noticed was the happiness in the people that I met. The happiest people were not the ones who were wealthy. The happiest people were the people that were surrounded by love and friendship. The nicest people around the world were the happiest and kindest ones, the people who were in touch with nature and in harmony with their minds.

I had seen that the world was not as morbid and serious as I had been led to believe, and in fact, it was actually filled with amazing human beings. I had met so many interesting people around the world from all walks of life, all of them with their own stories and bumps in the road that they'd had to get over.

The past few years, I had been surrounded by the most incredible people, and they had seemed to soften the war-hardened outer shell of this former sniper. Something that was a very scary thought for me at times, as I still held a lot of anxiety and felt unsafe a lot of the time.

My nightmares were not as regular anymore, but this in itself was a double-edged sword. Having fewer nightmares was great, but it meant that when they did come, they would terrify me. Which then, in turn, left me wanting to harden up my shell again, even though I knew that the way forward was for me to soften it further.

Meditation and mindfulness had played a huge part in my life for some time now, and certain places I had visited seemed to be just the perfect place to meditate or get in tune with the Earth. I remembered back to one time in California.

While sitting under a giant redwood tree, I felt this overwhelming connection with nature. I sat with my back against the tree, with my head tilted back looking straight up as far as I could see. The tree towered hundreds of feet above me, and it felt like the calmest place on Earth.

I sat and thought about how old this tree must have been and what it had experienced in its lifetime. I started to think about what wisdom the trees could pass on to humans if they could and how the universe would guide us if it could.

I began to meditate and quickly entered a deep state of relaxation. It felt as if the tree was taking away some of my negative vibrations and replacing them with positive ones.

I began to feel as though I was a small child, free from life's worries but vulnerable. This time, though, the vulnerability did not shake me; rather, it moved something within me. My vulnerability had allowed me, for the very first time, to feel compassion towards myself.

A single tear fell down my cheek as I nestled backwards into the tree and opened my eyes. The sky was blue, and the tree was warm against the back of my neck. The air was as fresh as I had ever felt it, and filled with the scents of pine needles and grass. It was a moment that I would recall again and again in the future when I needed to, and it was just what I needed to help right now.

Struggling for money and other typical life stresses seemed to start taking their toll on me quite quickly after I returned home. It seemed that day-to-day frustrations or anger would heighten the symptoms of my PTSD. The angrier or more stressed I became, the more the symptoms would increase, which then, in turn made me even more angry.

It was a cycle that needed to be broken. Otherwise, I knew my situation would begin to spiral. Months had gone by of working what was supposed to be just a temporary job from a friend. The workplace, however, was an overbearingly negative environment, and it was becoming detrimental to my mental health.

In an attempt to start on a new path, I had been asked to become part of a local non-profit organisation which was aiming to aid PTSD sufferers in their recovery.

I had recently made my thoughts known publicly about the astonishing rate of suicides by British soldiers, and this had gained me some attention from around the globe.

The number of British troops that had taken their own lives after the war in Afghanistan had now way surpassed the number that were killed on operations. The names were coming in multiple times a week through the British news media, and elsewhere around the world, figures soared to astronomical highs.

It was clear that there was a huge problem, and the National Health Service was far too underfunded to cope with the huge influx of mental health patients coming from the war.

A CAN OF WORMS

One afternoon, I sat down to meet with a member of the non-profit organisation, and in an attempt to put into words my experiences and thoughts, I began to speak.

The words fell out of me like a burst dam, my mind racing with images and memories that had not crossed my mind in a long time. I spoke firstly with confidence, as if telling a story I had heard a thousand times, but after a while, I began to stumble. The movies that took place in my mind had taken a strong hold of me, and as they increased in speed, my speech began to slow. A tug of war between reality and memory ensued, leaving me in floods of tears.

The experience left me shaken, but with a stiff upper lip, I continued to tell my story, in the hope that one day it might help somebody in need.

The thought of helping people spurred me on, and I thought back to how badly I needed to hear someone in my shoes speak about their situation when I was at my worst.

Later that evening I returned home, and I could not help but think about everything I had just spoken about. All of the new details that I could remember and the anguish that they brought flooded my mind. That night was a sleepless one as I tossed and turned until the sun came up.

I feared a relapse in my old symptoms more than anything; they had left me feeling a shell of my former self before and I was terrified to go back there.

Days went by of nothing but war filling my head, the sounds from deep within my mind were coming back.

It didn't take long for my PTSD to suffocate the life from behind my eyes or for the dark cloud of depression to descend upon me. Nightmares began to creep back into my sleeping hours, and flashbacks waited around every corner when I was awake. They would throw me around like a rag doll, powerless to when or where they would strike.

I tried my best to hide my symptoms, but just as my anger grew, so did the suspicion in the people around me that my troubles were back. I began to frantically grasp onto my sanity for dear life as my thoughts of suicide returned.

Suicide was like the ultimate off switch and the only thing that I was completely in control of. The idea that taking my own life was inevitable started to circulate around in my thoughts, and my violent temper had returned.

It hit me like a freight train, and I never saw it coming. Not too long ago, I was living a life of adventure that was almost too good to be true, and now I was back to wanting to die. There was no way I could continue my work with the non-profit like this, and so I withdrew from the organisation and back into the shadows.

As a result of me speaking publicly about PTSD and the current situation for veterans in the UK, I received many messages of encouragement and kind words. One of the people who contact me was a lady named Linda. From Austria, Linda was a deeply spiritual person who had deep routed ties to the world of holistic healing and meditation. She approached me from a place of care and compassion and kindly offered her help.

We began to talk daily over the telephone about my experiences and my thoughts. My thoughts would more often than not be negative ones, and they could go to extremely dark places. Linda helped me to rationalise my thoughts at times or would help me to see things differently if needed.

She was a strong woman who had a wealth of knowledge about meditation practices and spiritual lifestyles. Me myself I had experienced extraordinary things through meditation, but in order to fully submerse myself in a life choice that would test me to no end, I would need guidance. Linda would guide me through meditations while leaving positive suggestions like a trail of bread crumbs through my mind.

Together, we pulled apart all of the thoughts and thought patterns that I had. For instance, a good day would have to start with a good morning. The second I woke up in the morning; I would be in either a good mood or a bad one. This was mostly down to nightmares from the night before, but if a day started out bad, then in my mind, it was ruined. Linda would challenge me to think deeper into this kind of thing and say to me, 'Is it a bad day? Or is it something coming up to the surface that you must face?'

PTSD had humbled me. I thought I was invincible, after all, I had proved my theory so far. But the reality was that it had shaken me to my knees and left me somewhat unsure of who I was.

There was a disconnect between emotions and empathy, especially towards myself. One day, I would feel like a tiger trapped inside a cage that had given up on ever being free again. Then other days, I would be so filled with rage that the only thing I could do was punch the walls that surrounded me. My anger was a very serious problem, and it was reaching dangerous levels.

I was angry at everything. I was angry at the Taliban. I was angry at my own government. I was angry at myself. I was angry at the thought of the entire fucking war in Afghanistan being for nothing. I was angry that I had lost friends, and I was angry at myself for not being there to save them. I was angry at myself for being weak. I was angry about what I was putting the people around me through. I was angry that I was no longer the hero that I used to feel like.

I was angry that the only way I would be able to save myself would be to completely dedicate everything to change.

My anger came from many places, and a big part of tackling the problem was to start owning my actions and by being responsible for my behaviour. I began to make journal notes about each day, and how my mood was on that day. It gave me something to look back on and see if any patterns emerged. I noticed that on days where I did not accept the fact that I had PTSD or accept the things that I had done in Afghanistan, those days would usually be a bad day.

I started to notice that on days when I was moody or angry, I had absolutely no compassion towards myself or my situation. I would feel like I deserved everything I was getting after taking so many lives in Afghanistan.

Linda would get me to imagine that it was someone else that was experiencing these things, and how I would feel and act towards that person. I just could not comprehend that I was injured. 'You don't send wounded people to help wounded people,' Linda would say.

I felt overwhelmed with guilt and shame for what I had done, and although it was war, I just could not shake the fact that they were real people's lives that I had taken.

They weren't targets, or even just 'Taliban'. They were men that had been told certain things in order to make them do the bidding of others. Told a narrative that would shape them, a narrative that would create a preconceived path in which their lives should take.

Just as I thought about my own narrative and how stories or news media from around the world had persuaded me into my own military career, and steered me away from the life of a musician. Years of conversations and movies had led me to my dream of becoming a sniper, and the idea that it could have all been under false pretences was a tough pill to swallow.

Although I had the fight within me to accept the mammoth task ahead of me, there was a huge fear that I might not actually be able to shake this off. So, with nothing to lose, I jumped in head first and began to tackle my first hurdle.

I spoke in depth with Linda about every element of the lives I had taken. What they looked like, how they acted, and what was going through my mind at the time. I spoke about how it felt to pull the trigger and end someone's life. I talked about how the feeling was addictive in a way. I spoke about the intricate details in the final moments of the men's lives that I had taken. How some were terrified in their final moments, or how some seemed to be unequipped for the battlefield. How some fought until the very end, and how some seemed to accept their fate while surrounded by their own dead friends. The scenes that were left in my mind were more than just scenes from a movie. They were movies of what I had done and what I was responsible for, and they had a world of emotions attached to each and every one of them.

I was responsible for taking the life of someone's son, brother, or father. I was responsible for taking away someone's best friend or mentor. To be a sniper means to carry a heavy personal burden, and my burden was starting to pull me under.

FORGIVENESS AND ACCEPTANCE

Linda and I would talk for hours about how all of these things would make me feel, and we began to talk about a forgiveness meditation. The idea would be that she would talk me through a guided meditation, in which I would reach out to the souls of those I had killed.

To me, it was not an unreasonable thing to think that our souls move on once we are dead, and with that, I began to think that I had killed the bodies of those men, but not the souls. Through my spiritual mindset, I believed that our souls come to Earth for an experience, be that what it may.

I also believed that souls would surely hold no judgment and that the idea of being able to apologise for what I had done would maybe bring with it some relief.

Soon enough the day came to give the forgiveness meditation a go, and Linda called me so she could guide me through the experience. I quickly entered a calm, meditative state in which I began to visualise a cosmic space. Linda spoke over the telephone quietly, talking me deeper into a trance-like state and encouraging me to stay calm and breathe. I began to envision the men I had killed, and began to view the cosmos as a never-ending network in which I could call out to them.

With slow, deep breaths, I tried to send my frequencies to meet with those of the dead men. This was by no means something that I believed to be real, but I had to commit to the process as if I believed it to be fact. Linda's voice was now at the very edge of my consciousness, and as she faded further and further away, they started to appear.

Flashes of what I had seen through my sniper scope ran through my mind's eye, and the sorrow I felt with each vision only grew in its intensity. I felt as if I was beginning to connect with the souls of the lives I had taken, and the emotions bubbled up within me.

Linda encouraged me to send my emotions out to the universe and let the entities know my true feelings. I apologised wholeheartedly to the cosmic beings, and for just a moment, I felt like my messages had been received.

Suddenly, my heart rate started to rise, and the steady control that I had over my breathing began to slip, and I started to hyperventilate. Floods of emotion washed over me, and my hands began to frantically shake.

I was having a panic attack, and it was strong enough to drop me to my knees, and to make matters worse, I was home alone. Linda sprang into action, and quickly managed to talk me down and help me retake control of my breathing.

It took a couple of days for me to fully recover from the ordeal, but something inside of me felt different. Almost as if a weight had been lifted from my chest that allowed me to take an ever so slightly deeper breath.

My intention was not to receive forgiveness from the dead but to forgive myself and, more importantly, to accept the responsibility and the repercussions of my actions. It was not that I felt I had done the wrong thing, but it didn't feel like the right thing either.

The meditation had made me feel somewhat different, though, like I had put everything on the table for the universe to see, and it felt good to have apologised for the pain I had caused.

I knew that I needed as much help as I could get if I was going to squash my PTSD symptoms, and the holistic approach was not my only one.

Once my symptoms had reached a serious level, I wasted no time in contacting the Veterans Wales service. I knew just how dangerous my mind could be and just how fast it could deteriorate, and I knew now just how important it was to ask for help. The typical squaddie mentality is to grunt and get on with it, but time has shown that the typical mentality was not working.

The waiting list for an appointment was 12 months long, and that felt like light years away to me, which is partly the reason I submerged myself in holistic and alternative medication ideologies.

Throughout my years of suffering, I had always wondered about how humans had coped with the after-effects of war, be that WW2 veterans or the ironclad knights of Medieval times. I read about people atoning for their sins, mostly a religious-based idea, but it resonated with me. Priests would tell battle-scarred warriors that they could atone for taking the lives of others, and they would give appropriate lengths of time to atone for each kill.

By this point, it had been ten years since I had been diagnosed with PTSD, and often, during that time, I had felt as if I was serving some kind of punishment sentence. The past ten years had seen me mentally abuse myself, with a relentless bombardment of hatred towards myself, there was no way I was going to let myself off easy for what I had done. So, with now learning about the atonement that was advised in centuries gone by, I felt as though that is what I had been doing in a sense.

The months went by of my work with Linda, and the broader world of healing had started to reveal itself. The only options for help via the British NHS were antidepressants and therapy. Therapy was still some months away, and although I was doing as much as I could myself, it was clear to me that there were other options out there.

Alternative medicines were gathering astonishing momentum around the world, and the data was showing mass improvements in PTSD patients who had used the various alternatives. One such natural medicine was DMT, or N, N-Dimethyltryptamine. A sacred potion from the jungle tribes of Peru, DMT is the active ingredient in Ayahuasca.

Cannabis was already playing a role in my life for its medicinal properties, but it was not going to cure my PTSD. Cannabis allowed me to go deeper into meditations, helped to reduce the number of nightmares I had, and allowed me to think logically about my problems and be able to stay calm enough to do the work I needed to do inside of my mind. However, DMT was a far different thing altogether, and stories throughout history had told of its healing properties.

DMT AND PSILOCYBIN

The small living room was dimly lit as the smoke from the incense stick burning on the coffee table drifted through the air. Me and two of my veteran buddies sat anxiously as we tried to calm ourselves into a meditative state.

We were about to partake on one of the oldest rituals known to man and head out on a journey of learning and direction. DMT is derived from a certain tree bark, and as the concoction was being prepared, we sat in silence, and set our own personal intentions for the experience.

I had many thoughts and apprehensions about what I was about to experience, but I knew that the ritual could potentially help me to recover. The DMT was in powder form and had been rolled up into a cigarette.

In order for the chemical to reach the desired effect, we had to make sure that our minds were in the right place and also that our bodies felt completely relaxed. After a quick stretch, I sat on the sofa, the nerves vibrating inside of me.

It was my turn to smoke the substance, and it would not take much for the drug to take effect. I lifted the cigarette to my lips and took a long drag, filling my lungs with smoke. The first thing I noticed was the smell and the taste of the DMT; it was like nothing I had smelled or tasted before.

Instantly I began to feel lightheaded, and my vision began to blur. It was imperative that I didn't stop, though, and so after exhaling the thick white smoke of the first drag, I inhaled the next.

I sat back on the sofa as a warm wave of relaxation washed over me. My body felt as though it was in slow motion, and the blurry vision now seemed to have changed. As if reality was being peeled away in front of me, the room began to darken in spots around me.

It had started to become difficult to move my body by now, but I raised my hand to my mouth to take the final toke. For the final time, I took a deep breath in and held it, ensuring that I held in the smoke for as long as I could.

The room around me was silent, with everyone there to look out for each other as we went through the experience. I felt safe, and with that my head fell back to the sofa cushion. My eyes struggled to stay open as a hot patch began to grow on the back of my neck and head. A high-pitched ringing sound began to get louder and louder in my head just as colours began to appear.

Faint colours, like drops of water paint, started to appear, and an overwhelming feeling fell over me. It felt like my grasp on reality was about to be lost as a feeling of travelling through the air began to build. As I felt my body fly through the air, a road began to appear in front of me, not too dissimilar from a rainbow.

The road was made up of radiant colours and seemed to bend off to the left exponentially. The speed at which I was now travelling had reached astronomic levels, and the curved road was now just a blur. As the speed increased, so did the heat at the back of my head and the ringing in my ears. Just at the point where I could stand no more, everything stopped.

A flash of light and the ringing faded away, and I found myself once more floating out in the cosmos.

I was no longer a human being, I no longer needed to breathe, I just existed in the nothingness. Though the idea of being suspended in outer space would be a terrifying one, it was quite the opposite. I felt nothing but love and acceptance and a strange feeling that this place was familiar to me, like I had been there before.

Suddenly, from behind me, I felt a presence, as if a being had come to that place to meet with me. Without seeing the entity, I could feel that it was a soft, caring, womanly being that meant me no harm.

Telepathically, she began to communicate with me and gently awoke me to the ways of the universe. She knew why I was there and what troubled me. She knew everything about me, and without words but rather a feeling, she began to guide me on a journey through my mind.

Just off in the distance, I could see that the bright lights of the rainbow road had begun to fade back into sight. This time they were separated and had started to form individual clouds of energy and light, and they were enticing me towards them.

The female entity stood by my shoulder and somehow seemed to reduce me down to a tiny bullet-sized orb of light, and without another word, she sent me soaring through space. I hurtled toward the clouds of energy and light, and then I heard her voice.

It seemed as if light speed had been reduced to slow motion as the lady explored the emotions trapped within me and began to explain that the clouds were, in fact the energy sources of the people I had killed. The thought sent fear racing through my being as I grew closer to the pulsating colours.

A montage of gun blasts and deathly screams ran through my mind like a reel of cinema film. The voice reassured me that everything would be fine and that this was something I needed to face whether I liked it or not.

As I reached the first cloud, it revealed to me who this person was, and as if bracing for an impact, I gritted my teeth. Suddenly, a magnificent feeling of peace engulfed me, and with it came a stop to the replaying motion picture.

There was nothing but peace and tranquillity inside of the cloud and a relieving feeling of forgiveness. It was as if the idea that I had killed the bodies but not the souls was true, and the souls forgave me for my actions on the battlefield.

My light flew from cloud to cloud, energy to energy, and with each one, I felt more and more forgiveness. It was overwhelming, but the experience was short-lived, and soon, I had returned to where I had started, next to the womanly figure. The experience had been a humbling yet comforting one, and just as the subtlest of hints of reality began to appear, the entity filled my mind with what seemed like every piece of knowledge in the universe.

However, as I began to regain consciousness and be placed back into my body, all of that information simply faded away.

As my eyes slightly opened, and my body vibrated to the sound of a sound frequency that the group had been playing the entire time, I focused my vision. There sat Jay and Jonny, and the only words that I could muster were, 'What the fuck, mate?' The effects subsided, and something felt different. As if my mind had been cleaned, and for the first time in a long time, I was once more happy to be alive, for weeks after the experience, I could only see positive things in the world around me, like my world was being seen from a totally new perspective.

The DMT had lived up to its reputation and, without a doubt, had a life-changing effect on my quality of life. It also confirmed some of my thoughts about natural alternative medicines. Around the world people had been using natural medicines and ritualistic potions since the beginning of time, and there was another of these medicines that intrigued me.

The world of 'magic mushrooms' was a vast one, with multiple strains of mushrooms with multiple effects. The 'Liberty Cap' mushroom was one of the more potent strains, and it just so happened to grow wild in the hills of Wales.

The idea of using the mushrooms was to micro-dose the psilocybin to do multiple things. One was to increase and stabilise my mood, and the other was astonishing to scientists around the globe.

They had found that psilocybin had the ability to create new neurological pathways in the brain, essentially meaning that instead of our brains using the same route they had always taken or learnt to take in order to make decisions or engage with emotions, it could create new ones which could amount to different outcomes, like not becoming so easily angered for instance.

As much as the idea seemed inviting to me, I was not yet ready to take action. The seasons had twice changed by now, and my appointment with the NHS Veterans team was imminent.

BACK TO THERAPY

One morning, a letter came through the post, marked with an NHS stamp. I eagerly opened the envelope and began to read the letter inside. The letter gave me the time and location of my first therapy session, which sent a sinking feeling through my body.

A part of me felt as if I had taken a giant step backwards, and I felt like a failure. The idea of going back to therapy was a scary one, and I knew that it was going to bring the very worst of my PTSD bubbling to the top.

I had to be brave enough to stand toe to toe with my demons, and that included the monster that I had become in Afghanistan that still dwelled deep within me. Therapy was going to be tough, but I wasn't just doing it for myself, I was doing it for those around me, and to banish that doctors voice in my mind telling me I would be like this for the rest of my life.

The letter did, however, bring some comforting news to me. The therapist that had been assigned to work with me throughout my sessions would be Doug from all those years ago.

The appointment was soon now, but I had waited for so long that I had built the appointment up to become a very daunting thing inside of my mind. The anxiety I felt about therapy seemed to heighten my PTSD symptoms further, and so, really, the appointment could not come soon enough.

I was to meet Doug at a hospital an hour's drive away, in a small spare room of a hospital wing dealing with limb amputations. It wasn't the ideal place for vulnerable war veterans with mental health issues to be going for therapy, but Doug had been sure to call his patients before their first meeting to warn them of any potential triggers they may encounter.

On the drive to the hospital my mind was racing, overrun by thoughts of what I was about to face. I sat in the hospital car park and smoked one cigarette after the other before I could gain the courage to get out of the car. I walked towards the hospital doors and took a deep breath, when from behind me I heard a voice.

'Hello Ted, it's good to see you again. Shall we go in?' It was Doug, and he had been waiting outside for me to arrive to show me where the room was. 'It's good to see you too, mate, shit circumstances though, which is a shame,' I replied, and I followed Doug to the back office.

'Take a seat there for me, Ted, please. Do you want a brew?' 'That's a pretty good start to therapy,' I replied. 'Yes, please.' It was a strange feeling seeing Doug after nearly a decade, almost like seeing an old friend that you had to be at a professional distance from.

'OK, so can you tell me about what's been going on a little, and then we can go from there,' Doug said, and with a quivering bottom lip, I began to speak. I went on to tell Doug all about what I had been experiencing, from the nightmares to the most bizarre of thoughts. I spoke in depth about just how sad I had been feeling and how things like my anger were simply ruining my life, and there just seemed to be no getting away from any of it.

Therapy sessions were only roughly an hour long, so there was never going to be enough time to cover everything in the first session. However, it felt good to talk openly about my feelings with someone, and I left the session feeling slightly lighter than I did walking in.

It was hard to go back to therapy, but the best things in life are usually after doing something hard, and there was no question that I was going to do everything I could to get better. I continued to practice my meditation and mindfulness alongside with the therapy I was receiving from Doug, and that in itself had contradicting opinions.

Weeks went by of sessions simply consisting of me talking about my traumatic incidents and the demons they had brought with them. It was great that I could speak so openly about my problems with Doug, even some of the darkest of them all.

Doug had this way of making me feel comfortable and safe enough to speak my truth, no matter how horrific the graphic details would be. A bond was built between therapist and patient that encouraged me to not only put in the effort with my home assignments but to actually dedicate the time every single day to what Doug would suggest I do.

I had already dedicated much of my free time to holistic and spiritual practices, but the therapy and its significant homework would mean that most of my days and nights would be spent working on myself in one way or another.

DOING THE WORK

Going to war and staring death in the face daily, can break a person. However, it can also make a person realise that they can do anything, and that was just the mentality that I was starting to build.

I had never been an academic person or one for diaries or journals, so the idea that I now had to be attached to a notebook at all times was not a fun one. This was, however, the very definition of doing the work. I had to make these changes in my life; I saw it as though I had no other choice if I wanted to live.

I wrote thought diaries of everything significant that ran through my head in a day. I wrote about how these thoughts affected my mood and then what that led to. It began to show patterns to both myself and Doug, and it also brought to light some behaviours that I had.

Doug would call these learnt behaviours, such as parking the car somewhere that would enable me a quick getaway or leaving enough space between the car in front whilst driving for the same reason. Unreasonable thoughts and behaviours like having the curtains closed all day and night so as not to be seen by an enemy sniper or having to sit facing the door with my back against a wall when out of the house. These were things that had crept into my life over time, and they were significantly worsening my condition.

I would find myself staring into my own eyes in the mirror with pure hatred and anger or unable to walk down a busy shopping aisle due to crippling anxiety. These were things that I had to stop, and that is just what I did, as uncomfortable as it made me feel, I knew it was another victory that I must achieve.

Therapy was now well and truly underway, and after recollecting many of the events in Afghanistan, Doug had put forward a plan of action to me. The thought diaries, behavioural changes and constant self-assessment would continue as usual, and the next phase of the plan was known as prolonged exposure.

In one session, Doug had explained to me what he needed me to do, and it was not going to be easy. I got the feeling that this task would kick up some old dust that I did not want to deal with.

To engage with prolonged exposure therapy, I had a lot of work to do. For each event that had affected me in Afghanistan, I had to write out the entire experience in extraordinary detail from a first-person perspective. After writing out the event, I then had to audio record myself, reading out what I had written.

The idea was to expose myself by listening to the recording, sometimes up to ten times a day. After listening to the recording, I would then make notes of any changes within myself or things that I may not have thought about before.

Each week, I would present my notes and thoughts to Doug, and we would work through any points of interest or stuck points. Stuck points would be parts of the events which I would find most distressing or traumatic.

Another method of therapy that Doug introduced to run concurrently with the prolonged exposure was CBT. Cognitive behavioural therapy was another type of talking therapy that was aimed more towards the thought processes and behaviours that I was showing.

Doug would carefully listen to me talking about what had happened in Afghanistan and how it had affected me, but also the behavioural changes that PTSD had brought to my life, just like my driving protocols or scanning streets with hypervigilance.

Doug would point out any unhelpful or incorrect patterns or behaviours and then challenge me to face them head-on. These were things that I had been doing for years, and so the challenge was going to be a difficult one.

Months had gone by now of intense therapy with Doug, and already we were making some good progress on my mental health issues. And one thing in particular at this point was becoming more and more obvious to Doug.

I was not only suffering from PTSD, but I was also suffering from a lesser-known issue known as a moral injury. A moral injury was something usually involving betrayal, disproportionate violence, or a loss of trust. The idea was that I had rocked my core beliefs in doing what I had done in Afghanistan.

A person's core belief system is created at an early age, usually between the ages of three and seven. The core beliefs that I had made as a much-loved child from a safe and caring environment had led me to believe in certain things being good and some things being bad.

The monster that I had become whilst at war just simply did not correlate to who I was at my core. The moral injury diagnosis connected so many dots in my mind. I had always known that PTSD was not my only issue, and in fact, a lot of my symptoms and thoughts did not fit easily into the box of PTSD.

It reignited my curiosity in the history of combat-related mental health problems and also the stigma that had been attached to them. I read how the Christian crusade soldiers would hold one year of penance for each man they had killed, and that archers who had no definitive kill count would hold penance for three Lents. The thought was that these people needed to decompress and reconnect with real life and their loved ones.

Soldiers often believe that because they were trained to kill, the aftermath of doing so should not affect them, but this is quite simply unrealistic. WW2 soldiers who were experiencing mental health issues would often be referred to as hysterical or said to be having hysteria. At that time, the word hysteria was one in which to describe a 'woman's illness'. The term was intentionally used between the ranks to dissuade their soldiers from coming forward and presenting themselves as having a problem, and hence, the stigma was born.

The news of my new additional diagnosis was a welcome one, and I was keen to tackle the issue head-on. I still possessed that disciplined military mindset and would often try too hard to tackle my mental health, which would often lead to me constantly assessing myself and my head space.

The workload from therapy with Doug and Linda's spiritual work was taking up a significant portion of my time, and this came with its own stresses. It led me to a point where I was constantly angry and irritable from the non-stop replaying of scenes from my past. I needed a break or at least some way of cleaning up my mind.

The Liberty Cap mushrooms I had acquired had been stored away until the time felt right, and to me, there would be no more critical point of my therapy than right now, and so I decided to begin using the mushrooms.

By taking extremely small doses of the mushrooms a few times a week, I would build up a small amount of psilocybin in my brain. Within the first week I could feel the change, and most prominently in my daily mood level. Most days started with a low mood for me, however with the help of the mushrooms I was able to stabilise my mood to be more improved consistently throughout the weeks. Doug would talk about our brains having an imaginary stress bucket, and that when that bucket becomes too full, it overflows. The psilocybin seemed to reduce the amount of stress in my bucket, and in turn it allowed me to engage even further with my spiritual and clinical therapies.

Work with Linda was now heavily focused on my feelings towards myself and understanding some more of the spiritual methods that could potentially help me. The spiritual side involved imaginative practices, as did the clinical therapy, however, the more peace and love-based theories were making some significant changes in my life.

The inner child theory was one of the more powerful holistic experiences that I was made aware of and experienced. Just as the office clerk that lived inside your brain organising files and memories was a character of imagination, the inner child was another such character.

I would meditate with the intention of meeting with my inner child self. The idea was to be able to reassure the child that everything would be fine, that the bad stuff was over, and that everything was going to be OK.

The theory was that the toddler version of myself had also experienced the traumatic events, and they needed help from the only person who was able to help them, me. I would meditate regularly in an attempt to feel a connection with my inner child self, and after some time of doing this, I again felt a change in myself. So many positive changes were starting to happen that it seemed as if the stars were beginning to align. The idea that positivity attracted positivity was starting to make its way back into my life, just as it had done while travelling abroad. The meditation, the yoga, the breath work, the mindfulness, the alternative medicines, the spiritual guidance, cognitive behavioural therapy, the prolonged exposure therapy, the diaries and journals, and everything else was proving itself to be worth every minute.

With all of the journal writing and thought diaries, I had to give scores of my mood and anxiety. With the prolonged exposure exercises, I would score my anxiety before reading, during, and after. The numbers did not lie, and the data I had collected showed astonishing results and improvements. As well as the work from Doug that I was scoring, I had also begun to make note of my psilocybin amounts and score the effects it was having on me.

Nightmares had become almost non-existent, and the more I spoke out loud about the things that were was causing me problems, the easier it became to do so. Early on in therapy, I could hardly bear to think about the events, but now they didn't seem to bother me as much.

I was able to recall details about situations where my life was in imminent danger with little to no effect on my mental health. With such huge improvements in all of the multiple-choice questionnaire scores given to triage a person's PTSD, Doug decided that it was time to implement the final phase of his plan.

KEEP GOING

It had now been two years of me attending weekly therapy sessions with Doug, and it had been a testing time for both therapist and patient. I always thought about how my words may have affected Doug, and that he probably spent a lot of his private time thinking about ways to help his longest attending patient.

My mindset was now different, and the intense work I had done on my moral injury was showing. In order to heal my moral injury, I had to do many things. Acknowledgement of the transgression, a true expression of remorse, and a process of self-forgiveness and compassion would be the fundamentals of my recovery.

A large part of the therapy exercises would involve holding imaginary conversations with either a higher version of myself, fallen comrades, or someone who would be a respected moral authority in my life. The intention would be to image what these people would have to say to me about my thoughts and feelings, and to gain perspective, and internalise a compassionate voice within myself.

Understanding why I did the things that I did was another pivotal part in the success I was experiencing with my therapy. Understanding that sometimes good people do bad things, and also understanding the factors which played such a big part in my decision-making.

Doug suggested many real-world examples and experiments that showed just how people's decision-making can be altered. Lack of sleep, minimal food and water, pressure coming from within, pressure coming from peers, and pressure coming from commanders were all factors that played a part in my mindset. Research has shown that soldiers and their orders on the battlefield can play a part in moral decision-making and even allow people to do things they would not usually do.

All of these small details created a context that I could now use to see the events from different perspectives and actually believe that the way I saw things may not be solely my responsibility.

The past two years had taken me all the way from hating myself and the quivering wreck I had become back to being the happy, positive person I truly was deep down. As much as I was overjoyed with the progress I had made, there was still the final phase.

EMDR, or Eye Movement Desensitisation and Reprogramming, was to be the final type of therapy that I would do, and by this point, I was ready for anything.

EMDR was a therapy that was fairly new on the scene, yet Doug had studied the practice for some time. The aim was to help me fully process the traumatic memories that had haunted me for twelve years now. There were a few different options to tailor the method to my preference.

I would be asked to think about the events in which I had taken lives and try to recall as much detail as I could. While I was doing this, I would follow a light from left to right repeatedly with my eyes. The eye movement would replicate the movement made while a person is experiencing REM sleep. While in REM or Rapid Eye Movement sleep, the brain processes memory from left to right in the brain whilst storing the memory in the correct place at the back. EMDR had a great track record of helping people in their recovery, and I could not wait to get started.

The first EMDR session expectedly made me nervous, but both me and Doug had put a lot of time into preparing the exercise, and so we began.

I sat in the centre of the room with the white strip light standing opposite. The room was quiet and charged with energy as I took a deep breath and let Doug know I was ready.

I slowed my breathing and heart rate, just as I had done when preparing to take a life, and Doug's voice gently guided me into a deeply relaxed state. 'OK, Ted, slowly open your eyes for me and start following the light as it moves,' said Doug, and I began to follow the light with my eyes from left to right, right to left.

With very little encouragement, the first of many memories burst through to the front of my mind. My mind's eye began to take over my reality, and suddenly, I began to sweat. The incident with the enemy sniper holding siege began to play in my mind.

The session would be conducted in short one-minute intervals, and at the end of each mindful period, I would relay to Doug what had run through my mind. The idea was to not try and control the thoughts but just to notice them and see where they naturally go, almost drawing a map of my mind.

The sounds of the battlefield filled my head, and waves of images and emotions washed over me. The thought that I was about to die was a constant, and it was clear to see now why this had caused such a block for me.

Intertwined with the haunting footage were memories from completely unrelated things in my life. Childhood memories, good and bad, the faces of people from various times in my life, and thoughts that I had decades ago all ran through my mind. Doug would gently guide me through the emotions I was feeling and often make suggestions at the appropriate times.

The first EMDR session was a heavy experience, to say the least, and to my surprise, it had left me significantly shaken. The entire drive home that afternoon was a blur as I scrambled to make sense of what had just happened and what it all meant.

I had put in so much work over the past couple of years that when therapy punched me in the face one last time, I felt my mind wanting to resort to anger as the thing that would protect me. This time, however, my anger stayed locked away, and I began to genuinely see things differently. Of course, I was going to be upset, and of course, my mind was going to be running wild, and instead of being angry, I was compassionate and empathetic to myself.

It was the first time that it had happened, and it felt good. The tough, hard-man routine had gotten me nowhere and never would. It was the loving, compassionate side of living that held all of the greatest parts of life, so no more would negativity and anger rule my world.

The weeks went by, and with each EMDR session, it felt like I was gaining more and more knowledge about myself and how I could bring peace to my life once and for all.

Everything that I had learned and experienced over the past few years, from travel, to spirituality, to alternative medicines and therapy, had unshackled me from my demons and the traumas of my past. Every day was starting out better than the last, and slowly but surely, I started to let go of the constant self-awareness and criticism, and began to fully live my life in the moment, grateful to be alive. Triggers didn't trigger me, my anger had been tamed, my internal narrative was that of a happy man once more, and not a broken one. Everything was falling into place, and I finally learned to love myself.

I loved who I was; I was compassionate towards myself, and my music began to come back to life like a blossoming meadow of creativity. The cyclone that had whipped around my mind, destroying everything in its path, had finally passed.

It felt as if quite literal sunlight had burned away the darkest of clouds, ones that were suggested would never clear. I no longer welcomed death; I had a brand new life to live.

OUR SURVEY SAYS

I walked in through the hospital doors for the final time, and with a feeling of accomplishment, I sat in the waiting area.

'Ted, do you want to come in?' Doug said as he popped his head around the corner. He had a brew waiting on the desk for me and a stack of paperwork and folders. EMDR therapy had been a resounding success, and it was clear that this would most likely be the final time I would see Doug.

I had never been as grateful in my life towards somebody, for what Doug had done for me was truly astonishing.

In the last few weeks, I had been given questionnaires about my mental health. The multiple choice and numerical score sheets would gauge where I came on the PTSD scale. There had been a clear decrease through the weeks, and today, the final stack of test sheets would determine the final result.

I began to work my way through the papers, circling the appropriate answers to the many questions. Nothing seemed to apply to me anymore, and I was shocked by just how unwell I had been. I felt like a new and improved person, and it was as if I were filling out the forms on behalf of someone else.

I handed the papers over to Doug as I finished them one by one, and Doug sat quietly as he added up the scores. 'That's all of them, mate,' I said, and Doug totalled up the results of the entire stack of papers.

I sat patiently, and once I could see Doug had finished adding up the scores, I said, 'Right, come on then, mate. Am I still mad or what?' I could see a look on Doug's face that I had not seen before. Doug looked up slowly away from the papers, bewildered and turned to face me.

'This is amazing Ted. Your scores are showing that you don't have PTSD.' I jumped in the air and could not help but hug Doug and repeatedly thank him for everything he had done. It was a very emotional moment, and even Doug had a tear in his eye.

I said my final goodbyes to Doug, and as I left the treatment room and entered the corridor of the hospital, I couldn't help but feel like a free man. Smiling from ear to ear, I walked out of the hospital doors and got into my car. Tears of joy glazed my eyes as I sat there in reflection of the past 12 years. The highs, the lows, and everything that it had taken for me to reclaim my life.

Many people had helped me on my journey, and in my mind, I was so grateful to each and every one of them, but one person had been there and changed it all. The girl who had sat on the street with me while at my lowest. Fast forward a few years, and I married that life-changing woman, and we lived the happiest of lives together.

As the years passed by, the Welsh snipers' lives went in their own different directions. Dan continued his career in the Army where he became the Sniper Platoon Sergeant, started a family, and got married. Gray also stayed in the Army, and started his own family and married. Jenks emigrated to China after leaving the Army not long after returning from operations in Afghanistan. Bennie also left the forces not long after returning from Afghanistan and moved back home to start a family.

REFLECTION

Therapy was a complex and testing experience, and for the most part it frightened the life out of me, and the past couple of years seemed like a bit of a blur. I could feel that I was different, but there was so much information to process that it took quite some time for everything to settle into place.

Finally my mind was free of its shackles, and I was able to reflect on what I had achieved, and just what the stacks of papers and notebooks I had accumulated through the process actually meant. I had been meticulous with keeping notes from my sessions with both Doug and Linda.

Living with PTSD had affected me in so many ways, and addressing the issues had taken everything that I had to give. At times it felt like I was walking a tightrope toward regaining my sanity, and the fear of falling back into the blackness was far too much to bear. As I pushed deeper into my own mind, it revealed hidden thought processes and behaviours that had been slowly growing within me for quite some time. There were so many of these little things that they actually seemed to have been keeping my PTSD alive, or encouraging it to take hold of me with ease.

The way that Linda had challenged my thoughts had enabled me to see these issues from a different perspective. Things like 'having a bad day' would be questioned. Was it a bad day, or was it something just coming to the surface, that was providing an opportunity to be looked at?

It is important to accept, while suffering with a mental health issue, that there will always be ups and downs throughout life. That constant wave of ups and downs will just become less extreme at the end of the recovery road.

I seemed to grasp on to the idea of constant happiness as if it were a realistic goal, and this brought its issues. Having that ideology had meant that a 'bad day' was so much more than that. It was a step in the wrong direction, and possibly the first step in many, that would lead back to the darkest times of my life. This would terrify me, but that constant search for happiness also helped to pull me through the darkness.

Living with PTSD seemed to go in circles, and for years I seemed to have almost a calendar of emotions through a year, and I would know when the bad times were coming. Without realising, my brain was keeping track of dates and anniversaries of things that had happened. Sometimes they would be of things that had happened in Afghanistan, and sometimes they would be from the many anniversaries of friends who had passed. These anniversaries would send me spiralling down into a depression that could sometimes last for months and months of relentless mental turmoil.

It was the small but significant changes to my mood that became a bigger problem than I thought. Snappy and aggressive reactions would seem to appear from nowhere, or at least I thought. I was mostly unaware of the irritable mood that I mostly lived in. It was at times like this that I had to listen to those around me, and humble myself enough to agree with them. Often a snappy reaction would stem from something much deeper and this was easy to see from an outside perspective, but not from my own. It was only with time and patience towards myself that I would be able to look inwards in search of the true reason for my outbursts.

It became important for me to recognise and celebrate my successes, however small. If I found compassion towards myself, and actually saw myself as someone struggling, then that was a success. If I apologised for my angry outbursts rather than just leaving it to fester, then that could be deemed a small success. Completing small tasks throughout the day would give me a small feeling of accomplishment, and all of those small wins began to add up.

One of the more tricky tasks was that of balancing my mood. From anger, anxiety, depression to fatigue, I had to constantly be in a state of awareness, and use the skills I had learnt in order to balance my mood like a spinning plate on a stick.

My own imagination would be able to put me in a bad mood just by thinking about pulling that trigger, I would snap into a callous mindset. Sometimes to feel the way I used to feel on the battlefield, and sometimes just to get through the day. My anger, however was an outdated version of myself, and I knew it.

Anger had become my default setting, and with good reason. Anger had kept me alive, and it was like comparing a motorway to a long winding country road. It was easy to be angry and careless, but it was hard to be positive and caring. At times it felt like I had lost myself, and was going through a crisis of identity.

It was important for me to listen to my body, and take stock of my energy levels, and to spread my energy equally. My energy levels were unstable, and depending on my state of mind, some days would be simply exhausting. These exhausting, tough days, however, were important as they gave an opportunity to learn what worked for me.

There were many things that helped, from music and painting, to exercise and meditation, or even just a simple phone call. Being able to talk to someone over the phone would always change my state of mind, and it became apparent just how important it was to talk about my problems. In some ways I didn't trust my own mind, and with good reason. My mind was a dark place at times, and things became easily twisted or distorted.

The concept that my mind was like a pressure cooker was one in which I could get behind. The heat beneath the cooker was fuelled by anger and hatred born from my experiences in Afghanistan. Being triggered by things would only add to the fire, and so it was important for me to begin trying to take things less personal. Day-to-day grievances could be responsible for days of anger, and it was quite simply time to let go. By doing this, I could remove the heat from under the pressure cooker and physically feel the relief. Another way for me to lift the lid and release some pressure was to do one of the many things, like a phone call or music, that would bring about a positive change in my mood.

The complexity in which PTSD would operate in my mind took immense patience and self-reflection in order to begin to understand. So many feelings and emotions were piled on top of each other that it was hard to decipher what was what. In order to do so, I began to trace my thoughts, decisions, and influences from throughout my life.

For some reason I just could not shake the feeling that I had let people down, made a fool of myself, and was embarrassed to have a mental health condition. Casting my mind back through life events began to give me context, something that played a huge part in my therapy.

The context, and reality of it all was that I was a nice guy, who was loving, outgoing and always happy. So what was a person like that doing in a war zone, taking life after life? It was a culmination of many factors, some close to home, and others that were plastered everywhere I looked by the media. Terrorism was the word of the day, and somehow this group of people I had never heard of had become my mortal enemy.

Context was king, and seeing things with that in mind was a game changer. I saw how I had been moulded, and I saw how I had encouraged my own mind to be that of someone capable of doing what I would later do. I was able to look back and see clearly the things that had changed me, and just how it all began to fall apart. I put incredible pressure on myself on behalf of other people, and encouraged anger to live just beneath the surface.

My time in Afghanistan had made me hyper vigilant, and that in itself was an exhausting factor in my day-to-day life, bringing constant triggers and waves of emotion.

I learnt that it was important for me to stabilise my mood before doing anything in the mornings in order to best prepare me for the day's challenges. I learnt that I often felt numb, and would invoke anger by picturing events from the war just to feel something. Daily journals would allow me to strategically look back at my moods and the thoughts which affected them. There were always patterns, and in learning those patterns I was able to redirect my anger into something productive, and sometimes even avoid a potential mood change all together by pre-empting my triggers and preparing for them.

It was a delicate balance between listening to my body when it was tired, and pushing myself towards recovery, that took up most of my drive in life. It tested me beyond anything before, and it also tested those around me.

Little knockbacks were devastating for years, and then with simply allowing myself to feel the hurt I had inside, and not fight against it, it all became easier. Instead of seeing myself as weak, I began to see my true self inside that needed help. Having a bad day wasn't the end of the world, frustrating as it was, the best thing I could do was to just let myself go with the current.

Often I would burn out due to the sheer amount of effort it would take to hide my true feelings from people, but once I learned to be open about it all, I no longer had to hide. I realised that I didn't need to hide how I felt from the people around me, but rather I should let them in and hear what they have to say.

It felt like so much of my life had been ripped away from me that I refused to let it happen again, and the only way I could do that was to be honest to myself and those around me about my thoughts and feelings. It allowed me to preserve my energy, and actually enabled me to see further into the concept that context was everything.

A person's moods are like the weather in that they are constantly changing, and so if a low mood would overcome me, it was best for me to just go with it and let people know that was my current state. I was resisting reality by trying to fight my mood, and I was never going to win that fight. I had to listen to the call that I needed to rest, and that sometimes I had to be alone. This would sometimes worry me as I saw it as a red flag to anyone around me, which meant they may be left walking on eggshells. However, with my newly gained perspective on life, I began to think that maybe me taking myself away quietly was giving the message that I was going away to do what I needed to do in order to fix things so that people did not have to walk on eggshells around me.

These walk-away moments could often lead to inward anger in the past, and I would find myself resorting to that callous military mindset. The fact of the matter was though, that the military mindset was not helping me, and didn't seem to be helping anyone else I knew that was struggling with their mental health either. I had to realise that I was not who I was in the Army, that was a trained state of mind, and not that of my true nature. I needed to reconnect with who I truly was, and humble myself.

It was important for me to be aware of my inner monologue, that voice inside my head that had been so destructive in the past. As time went by this voice shifted from that of a pessimistic, angry person, to that of a happy one, content with his life and feeling at his best. This brought on the biggest change in my life, and soon I went from hating every single morning, to waking up excited for the day.

My experiences in the military had shaped and trained my mind in order to do the job, but once the job was done, it seemed that there was no going back. I would often feel guilt for shooting people, and would sometimes find myself imagining the fear and pain that someone being shot by a sniper would feel. There is, however, no place for those kind of thoughts in the Army, and in fact an emotional disconnect was created. People were targets, they were not seen as human beings. That disconnect allows soldiers to do what they do, however, for some they can never reconnect. I was reconnecting to my emotions, and it was at times like having to learn to ride a bike again. I dared to feel into the pain and suffering of those men I saw through my scope.

A lot of time was spent revisiting shots I had made, and it was at times useful. One technique Doug had me do was to play a video of the events in my mind, and just before the anxiety would kick in, rewind the video. Exposing myself to the events in a controlled manner was important, but it was just as important for me to talk about my reflections on the events. Be that with those close to me, or by using the empty chair technique where I would envision a conversation with someone I thought to be of a high moral standing.

I was advised to watch a documentary called 'The Five Steps to Tyranny'. A film that shows how good people do bad things. It was a light bulb moment, and floods of realisations washed over me as I began to make notes on my new thoughts. Another piece was being added to the puzzle, and it all started with 'us and them'. A mindset that had been drilled into us from all angles, starting with the news media, and culminating in army training.

Myself and the soldiers around me all hated the Taliban, even though they had no direct impact on our own lives before the war. There was a group mentality and there was a communal hatred that would only grow as the war progressed. Friends being killed, hearing about friends of friends being killed, these were both huge factors that fuelled the hatred and anger, and it gradually darkened the minds of the young Welsh troops with thoughts of revenge. It provided a strong motivator, but also began to blur the lines of moral integrity. These swirling emotions among young, violent men, who are constantly following orders, with the overall order consistently to defeat the enemy, and a mindset bursting with moral courage, was the perfect setting to create killers. The men wanted to fight, and they wanted to kill, and they believed that they were all doing the right thing. They had been drilled with moral integrity, and rather than stand aside, they would stand up and fight for what they had been made to believe, despite completely disregarding any thought of humanity.

Therapy and spirituality had both changed the way in which my mind was working, and they had allowed me to address issues which I never really understood. I understood my PTSD, but there was more to it, and the moral injury I had been diagnosed with was proving to be responsible for many of my problems.

One of the tasks that seemed to shine light on some of these almost hidden issues, was by writing out the various events in the first-person perspective. By then reading these memoirs over and over, I was able to pinpoint over time the feelings I had about what I was responsible for, and how the feelings I had in those moments had carried with me for years to come.

Thought diaries were without question one of the most empowering aspects of the recovery process. I would consistently have negative thoughts swirling around my mind, and although I felt I could manage to live with them, the detrimental effect that the day-to-day negativity was having on my mental health was far greater than I imagined.

First it was important to learn about the unhelpful thinking biases and patterns that were forming in my mind. These constant negative thoughts would impact my life every single day, and the relentless cycle would often cause my mood to plummet. These thought biases and negative thought patterns could manifest in many ways, and most of the time I would be oblivious to them.

Assumptions that my mind would make would appear as fact, things like overgeneralising. Assuming that something negative will happen or that an experience will be a negative one, because it has happened before. A mental filter would stop me from seeing the positives in my life, and instead only the negative would stick with me. Mind reading would cloud my judgement, by being convinced I knew the negative thoughts people had about me, I began to redirect that negativity to those around me.

Hindsight bias was the process in which I would look back on the events from my past and condemn myself with what knowledge I currently possessed. I would constantly ridicule my actions, how I had taken men's lives, but the fact was that again, context was crucial. This type of self-critical thinking became my greatest tormentor. Having a constant self-expectation of toughness had created what was known as an inner bully. That internal monologue with its constant pushing and poking was enough to drive a man insane. There was nothing I could do right, and with every dressing-down that I received from that voice in my head, my mood would worsen further. This would initiate the vicious cycle of shame, guilt and anxiety that would grow exponentially.

Black and white thinking would make me assume that everything was either good or bad. There was no in between, there was only right and wrong. A stern, callous outlook on life was the last thing I needed, but my emotions were so clouded and confused that life felt hopeless. My anxiety would often leave me feeling as if I were in imminent danger, and this could often bring with it some very nasty adverse reactions.

By feeling a constant threat of danger, I would often be just a sudden loud noise away from hurtling back in time and reliving my experiences in Afghanistan through flashbacks. A series of events had unfolded in my life that I just simply could not shake off, and it was the only thing I could think of.

Rumination was the name for what I was experiencing, constantly thinking about past events in order to reason with myself, punish myself, or to just hopefully come to some other conclusion. Never including new information or perspectives, for over ten years I went through the events over and over again in my mind, always coming to the same conclusions, and always feeling the same terrible sequence of heartbreaking emotions.

Worry would often rule my life, and at times be powerful enough to confine me to my bed for days at a time. Subconsciously my brain would believe that worrying was a helpful thing. It seemed that if I worried enough about everything, that I would be able to pre-empt dangers, or certain situations that may otherwise catch me off guard. A feeling of constant readiness was expected, something that again was more debilitating than at first thought. The amount of energy it took to constantly worry and overthink things was staggering, and the recurring question of what if would drain me to no end, and often lead to more intense anxieties and worry.

The thought diaries I wrote daily would consist of multiple columns. Situation, Negative Thoughts, Emotions, Biases, and Alternatives. The situation column would be for writing out what had happened that day to evoke negative emotions, be that a real life event or a product of my mind casting itself back to Afghanistan. The Negative thoughts column would be where I would write the thoughts that followed the event, be that a road rage incident from that day that had caused anger, to an intrusive thought of pulling that trigger so many years ago. The latest goings-on in Afghanistan were at this point very prominent in the news media, and hearing about the loss of ground now retaken by the Taliban would often cause a rage inside of me. It was in these moments that I had to see them as a positive opportunity to collect insights to aid my recovery. A whole range of thoughts would race around my mind, mostly negative ones which brought about negative emotions and even at times thoughts of suicide. The inner workings of my traumatised mind were complex and powerful, but by simply writing down my thoughts and feelings I was able to later decipher their meanings and use them to my advantage. I would score my emotions numerically, and over time I was able to simply read where and when things were going wrong.

The emotion column of the thought diary would be to place every emotion I felt from the situation. More prominent than most was the overwhelming feeling of guilt and shame, but this was all useful information to me. The next column was for thinking biases. This took some practice, but the idea was that I could look back at my reactions and thoughts, and then start to see how the negative thinking patterns and biases I had were affecting my life. By being able to see how I had used a mental filter to only see the negatives, or being able to see how my black and white thinking had affected myself or those around me, I was able to begin the long process of changing my ways.

The final column was for the alternatives section, and this was the part in which I struggled most. The alternatives to my emotions were hard to see, and with good reason. My life had been about the negatives for so long, and being in that state of mind for such a long time was difficult to shake.

Often I would perceive myself as a bad person, however, the alternatives column would prove otherwise. If I were this bad person that I perceived, then I would not feel bad for the things I had done. If I were an evil monster inside, then why would I cry for those I had killed? These empowering realisations over time began to grow, and very slowly things began to change.

My negative outlook on the world began to shift, and I began to forgive myself for what I had done, and the culmination of an astonishing number of factors began to set the wheels in motion towards my recovery. By being able to look back at months of thought diaries and the emotional scores I had given, I was able to see that I was in fact making progress, and I began to believe in myself once again. Seeing how my outward reactions were changing, and how my temperament was changing too showed me little glimpses of the person I used to be. I was beginning to understand my actions, the effect they had on those around me, and in turn the effect that they were having on myself. I was getting in my own way, but my true self was starting to shine through, and with that I began to feel happy once more. By no means was this the end, but it was the first time that I had felt like myself in a very long time.

There were various unhelpful mindsets which seemed to come as part of the package with PTSD, and these were very difficult to spot at times. The protector mindset would often leave me feeling responsible for the safety of those around me, which in turn would add to my already heavy load. I had to learn to drop my being prepared for anything mindset, after all, it was simply adding fuel to the fire. Constantly assessing threats was exhausting, and it was time for me to let go. That military mindset was no longer helping me, and by now I had realised that it never went down too well with those around me anyway. I had to have a mindset of self-compassion, and allow my defences to drop. I was no longer the person I once was, and that was OK.

One significant task that I completed towards the end of my time in therapy was to write about my identity. I wrote about the person I would like to be, the person I was, and the person that I would like people around me to see. It allowed me to see the negative aspects of my life that needed to be dropped, and the positive aspects of my life that I wanted to keep.

I was regaining my life piece by piece, and it felt amazing. I knew where my problems came from, I knew how I had kept them alive for so many years. I knew how they had changed me, but now I knew that after everything I had been through, it had made me a better person.

I had evolved mentally and spiritually, and although these aspects had both helped to save my life, it was also important that I did not maintain the constant assessment of my mental state, and instead let everything go in order to move forward with my life. I could now look back at my younger life with a smile on my face. I had experienced incredible things all over the world, and held cherished memories.

I had learned to love, and to be loved. The love from my wife had ignited a long-extinguished flame inside my heart. At one time I felt as though I were already a dead man walking among the living, but now I was so full of life. I was grateful to be alive, and soon enough the past began to fade. I even began to forget, and as I sat writing this book, I smiled the whole way through. Sat there for over a year, I watched my wife from the other side of the room, and I knew it was all worth it just to be sitting here with her, and our little dog curled up beside me.

INDEX

Military Terms and Concepts
  Armoury 90–4
  Ballistics 23, 92
  Camouflage 10–11
  Escape and evasion 9, 12–13
  Final fire position 19, 14–17
  Ghillie suit 11
  L96 rifle 2, 17, 30, 58
  Night navigation 20–1
  Observation 14–18
  Precision shooting 15, 23
  Reconnaissance 53, 71
  Sniper training 33, 119
  Stalk 14–19

Places
  Afghanistan 47–89
  Brecon (Wales) 9–21
  Brisbane 125–32
  Camp Bastion 54–71
  Canada 149
  Kenya 33–43
  Portugal 142–7
  Scotland 18
  Sydney 123
  The Farm 125–29

Combat and Deployment
  Enemy sniper 58–62
  Mobile Reconnaissance
    Force 53, 71
  One-mile shots 79–84
  Operation Moshtarak 71–78

Psychological Themes
  Counselling 109–65
  Fear 57, 95
  Forgiveness and acceptance
    163–9
  Mental health 95–169
  PTSD 95–109
  Resilience 122, 169–74
  Trauma 95–115
  Trust the process 113, 150–70

Recovery and Healing
  DMT 159–60
  Holistic healing 121–3
  Psilocybin 161–3

Culture and Life Beyond
  the Military
  Adventure 123–49
  Travel 142–9